ALLIED TO WIN

ALLIED TO WIN

How I Launched and Led a Leading
eCommerce Company

BY EDWARD STEVENS

San Luis Obispo

Editorial production by Lori Hobkirk at the Book Factory
Design by Anita Koury
Cover design by Pete Garceau

ISBN-13: 978-0-9911459-0-4
e-book ISBN: 978-0-9911459-1-1

All photos are from the personal collection of Edward Stevens.

Published by FirePoppy Press

For more information about this book, or to learn more about Shopatron,
visit www.shopatron.com, or call 1-805-547-8368.

10   9   8   7   6   5   4   3   2   1

CONTENTS

FOREWORD

Even though it was May, our water bottles had frozen during the night due to the unusually late winter that year. The Mount Whitney Trail (aka "The Backpacker's Route") was, during the clear days of summer, strenuous but decidedly non-technical. Today, however, it was completely frozen over with waist-deep snow covering the switchbacks winding up the seventeen-hundred-foot vertical cliff face. Ed and I, along with another rugby teammate, had decided a few weeks earlier to make a go at hiking up Mount Whitney, the highest peak in the lower forty-eight states. Coming off the season, we underestimated the challenge that its early season 14,494 feet would pose to us. As we turned on the stove to melt some drinking water and stomped our boots in an effort to get the blood flowing in the scarce light of dawn, we considered our predicament. After a long drive and hike to this point in our journey, we were not excited about turning around and facing the long drive home. The alternative was to somehow make our way up the snowy cliff face without crampons or ice axe, with slipping and falling a real possibility, and a bone-chilling slog certainly an inevitability. So we put our wool socks on our hands as mittens, drove our arms into the slope, and post holed up the face. Arms windmilling, legs sinking in the snow up to our waists, hands cramping into claws in the cold, we repeated to ourselves, "Don't look down, don't slip." A little more than one very frozen hour later, we were at the ridgeline enjoying the spectacular views across the Sierras and ready to thaw a bit on the rest of our amble toward the summit. In retrospect, it was a bit reckless, though the positive outcome made us glad we persevered.

Over the years, our paths diverged as Ed jumped headfirst into the world of entrepreneurship and I entered the more staid world of finance. We kept in touch periodically to trade ideas, and when Ed contacted us regarding a fund-raising process into which he was embarking, my business partner, Jay, and I leapt at the prospect of investing in Shopatron. The company vision—to facilitate commerce as the first truly multi-tenant SaaS (software-as-a-service) order management solution—was an idea that electrically and immediately hit me at both the cognitive and visceral levels as fundamentally right. The management, execution, and fulfillment of consumer product orders in "the cloud," regardless of the source of those orders, provide a real solution to a significant pain point to etailers, retailers, manufacturers, and distributors alike, and was a solution uniquely enabled by a multi-tenant infrastructure. Ed's execution of this vision began well before the current inexorable trend toward SaaS, and it was ahead of its time. According to comScore and other industry researchers, the rapidly growing U.S. eCommerce market will exceed $250 billion in 2013, while according to Gartner, the SaaS market will exceed $15 billion during the same period. My faith in this vision has only continued to grow since then, and I am extremely honored to work with Ed and his team.

A lot of ink has been spilled on the unique nature of the entrepreneur and entrepreneurship (much of it using the mountain as metaphor!)—the desire to build things; the ability to weather the nagging, lonely fear of failure while motivating others; prophetic insights into what new products or services that the world needs. These ring true for what I have seen among entrepreneurs, including Ed. One attribute shown by Ed stands out to me as particularly enjoyable: a deep engagement in the world around him as both observer and actor, coupled with an insatiable hunger to keep learning more. This attribute assisted us on our journey on Mount Whitney, and ironically, it is this same attribute that I feel makes great writers and great writing, including the book you now hold in your hands. If I had one piece of advice to add to Ed's many excellent points contained herein, it is that openness in communication, the ability to share ideas freely, faith in vision, and a mutual trust in each other's judgment is crucially important to foster a healthy relationship between an entrepreneur and his or her investor(s). It has been a joy to watch Ed grow Shopatron.

Part how-to manual, part picaresque, part biography, part thriller, Ed's book has something to offer both seasoned and new entrepreneurs, eCommerce professionals, anyone engaged the world of business, or interested in an individual's candid and personal journey.

I expect that you will enjoy reading this book as much as I have and share in our excitement for the future of Shopatron.

Here's to eCommerce, transformed!

J. P. Whelan, General Partner
Kern Whelan Capital, LLC

PREFACE

Someday, a consumer will be able to go on her computer or phone and—in a few seconds—locate every single product in every single store and warehouse in the world. She will be able to research the products and then buy whichever one she wants, whenever, and wherever: online or offline. When she buys it online, she will be free to have it shipped to her home or to have it available for pickup at the most convenient location of her choice.

No matter how obscure the product. Or how big or small. She can have it delivered her way.

Shopatron, one of the world's fastest-growing eCommerce companies, is making this dream come true. Our vision is simply this:

Any Product. Anytime. Anywhere.

That is the future we at Shopatron strive for today. Yet Shopatron has been over a decade in the making, and during that time I have learned a lot about building a technology company from the ground up. About sales, leadership, growth, change, and most of all, customer experience.

In the following pages I will share stories about Shopatron and myself— what I have learned on the path to creating a powerful new concept for delivering superior experiences to online and offline shoppers.

My personal and professional challenges have shaped Shopatron into the company it is today. If only one entrepreneur, investor, or student of business avoids one mistake by reading this book, it will be a success in my mind.

CHAPTER ONE
BEGINNINGS

You could say that I was born and bred to become an entrepreneur. Not a single one of my role models growing up had ever held an honest job working for a paycheck. Every one of my six uncles and both grandfathers ran their own businesses: furniture stores, machine shops, and restaurants. When our family gathered on Thanksgiving, these men would sit around the TV and pretend to watch football while they talked about the successes and failures of their latest ventures. When Uncle Ken's new furniture store in Akron went broke, he would tell us about it, without looking despondent or sad, and then wax on about the next business he was starting. When Uncle Ron drove up in a new Lincoln because he had a good year stamping auto parts for Ford, everyone went outside to hear him tell the tale and have a celebratory drive around the block. It never occurred to me that starting a business was a risky thing to do. Life went on, and we ate turkey regardless of the ups and downs.

As a thirty-two-year-old man with a wife and two kids, it was therefore surprisingly easy to get up the gumption to launch Shopatron. I had already followed in the family tradition with two business ventures of my own, and had been able to feed my family and buy a house (no-doc loan, of course).

Neither of those first two businesses were abject failures, but my celebratory drive around the block was yet to come. My first start-up was Most Atlantic Company, which imported and distributed underwater spearguns from 1993 to 1997. My second was Northern Velocity Ltd., later "Norvel," an importer and distributor of model airplane engines from 1995 to about 2003.

For both start-ups, I was sourcing products from Russia because I had lived there for a year after graduating from college (more on that later). Importing products from Russia not long after the fall of the Iron Curtain presented a challenge. I was required by law to put the country of origin on the imported products: Russia. The former Soviet Union. Other than Stolichnaya vodka, I am still not aware of a single Russian consumer brand that made it in the United States and stuck.

This led to my first lesson in launching a business: **To penetrate a market, you have to think big, be creative, and distinguish yourself from the competition.**

When it came to attracting the interest of American underwater hunters in a Russian speargun, I had a simple concept. Leverage the one thing in the world that was Russian, reliable, and famous (at least to hunter-types): the AK-47 service rifle. I choose the name "Seabear" for the brand to conjure the image of the cold war Russian bear. I chose a font that looked Cyrillic. With a tinge of nervousness that I might be doing something too cheesy and yet knowing that I had to do something edgy, I named our first model the AK-72.

After some initial testing in local dive shops, I learned the AK-72 was actually a decent spear gun. Typical of Russian weapons, it was easy to clean and maintain. It had plenty of power and a comfortable grip. All of these unique features were clearly stated in our advertisements.

Sure enough, customers noticed Seabear. Some joked about the cheesy reference when they learned there was no actual connection to Kalashnikov, the designer of the famous Russian AK-47 rifle. But what mattered was that people read our ads and bought our spear guns. My differentiation strategy worked.

Underwater hunting is a niche market inside the already-quite-niche diving equipment market. There wasn't enough opportunity in spear guns, so the guys at the Russian factory and I decided to add another product line to our import/export program. An engineer in the factory, who happened to be a model airplane enthusiast in his spare time, had designed some model engines. In an effort to grow non-military revenues, the factory decided to put them into production. Fortunately, model aviators care most about performance and price, and our engines were competitive on both counts. For eight years, Norvel made and sold model airplane engines in the United States and around the world.

My time building Norvel coincided with the first Internet wave, in the mid to late 1990s. I was in charge of worldwide marketing and sales and, as you might expect, Norvel was one of the first manufacturers in the hobby industry to have a website. It didn't take long to figure out that modelers loved going to the Norvel website to learn how to use their engines better. They also wanted to buy spare parts. That made sense, because even the deepest-stocking Norvel retailers had very few spare parts in stock.

Initially, around 1998, I did what any green-blooded American would do: open up an online store to sell my spare parts. That worked great for consumers, but it didn't work so great for my retailers. They did not like one bit the idea that Norvel was a direct seller of Norvel products. If a customer saw my products at the local hobby shop but then came to the Norvel website and bought them, the shop got screwed out of a potential sale. The local hobby shop added real value for Norvel—the ability for a customer to see and test the product, to talk to a knowledgeable salesperson, all of those things that make an in-store visit worthwhile—and yet got nothing in return.

I couldn't stop thinking about this problem. Part of me felt fine about this: Business is business. People get hurt. But there was a nagging feeling that I could do better, that I could find a solution that worked for everyone, that peace and harmony is more powerful than pain and friction.

I knew for an absolute fact that manufacturers face a dilemma when selling online. Consumers frequently want to buy on the manufacturer's site, sometimes because it's hard to find what they are looking for, but often just because it is faster and easier to buy online. But buying directly from manufacturers undercuts sales by retailers, and thus manufacturers can't sell directly to consumers unless they want to become competitors with their own retail partners. Being a competitor with a partner can work some of the time, but it definitely doesn't work over the long haul.

Then it came to me: Take the order a consumer places at the manufacturer website, but then send the order to a stocking retailer. The retailer can then make the sale and fulfill the order to the consumer. In that way, consumers could enjoy the convenience of buying from anywhere online while local retailers could still reap the benefits of the sale. This idea would be the basis for my third, and far and away most successful business, Shopatron.

The exact moment when I conceived of the Shopatron business model is long gone from my memory, but I know that, once the idea had formed in my brain, I could conjure up an adrenaline rush anytime day or night just by thinking about it. In fact, it's safe to say I couldn't get the idea out of my head.

Here's an example of how I imagined it would work (and how it does today).

Johnny goes into the local running-shoe store, gets his stride analyzed on the treadmill, and is custom-fitted for a pair of new running shoes. They happen to be Snakebrand shoes, because the guy from the shop tells Johnny they fit his stride the best. Johnny isn't sure his wife will let him spend $100 on a pair of shoes, so he tries to text her on his phone. No answer. She never answers her texts! Frustrated, Johnny leaves the store.

That evening, Johnny asks his wife about buying the shoes, and she gets all excited that he wants to work out. Maybe she remembers the days when he was hot and in shape. Johnny is pleased with her reaction and grabs his iPad and goes to the Snakebrand website. He buys the shoes the local running store recommended, in the size he needs.

Snakebrand sells him the shoes and ships them directly to Johnny's doorstep.

The local retailer set up a store, paid rent, hired the employee to fit Johnny for the shoes, and Snakebrand made 100 percent of the profit on the sale.

If the running-shoe store owner is paying attention, he might feel a bit disappointed in Snakebrand. He lost a sale to Snakebrand's own website because Snakebrand sells directly to consumers and does not partner with retailers on those sales.

Now if you take Johnny's scenario and plug in Herobrand running shoes instead of Snakebrand, the story would be the same all the way up to the point where Johnny goes home, gets his wife's enthusiastic approval to purchase, and then buys the shoes on the Herobrand website. Because Herobrand is powered by Shopatron, Johnny's order would be sent back to the local retailer, who would ship Johnny his shoes or invite him to come in and pick them up in store. Thus Shopatron offers a win-win solution where the local retailer does not lose sales to online orders, the manufacturer is able to make money without competing with its retailer, and the customer is happy because he made the purchase on his own time and according to his preferences.

Once the idea solidified, it took one full year for me to flesh out how I would actually make the whole thing happen. One year of driving home from work thinking hard about how to solve edge case after edge case of the solutions work-flow (answering questions like, what if no one in our network had the product in stock? what if a customer wanted to return a product?). One year of sitting on the couch at night, after putting my one-year-old son and three-year-old daughter to bed, catching the last few innings of the Indians or the end of a Cavs game, writing the specification for the software developers to build Shopatron. I had never designed a software program before, so I bought some books and cobbled together a flowchart and a database schema.

During this process, my wife and I decided to pick up and move our lives from Cleveland, Ohio, to San Luis Obispo, California. Robin was from California and wanted to go back. I thought California, where people were crazy enough to believe the world can change in leaps and bounds, would be a great home for a radical new idea.

We sold our house, rented a small, crappy one, and used the proceeds to build the first version of Shopatron. Despite the risks of pumping our future into the present, Robin could not have been more supportive. She was 100 percent on board for the adventure.

That was a good thing, for it took an unwavering commitment to my idea for Shopatron to survive the gauntlet of naysayers I encountered on the start-up path. People were telling me:

"You have absolutely no experience in the software business."

"More than 50 percent of new businesses fail."

"Somebody is already doing this."

"You have small children."

"You have no college or retirement savings."

"Get a regular job."

It all fell on deaf ears with me. This led me to lesson number two about launching a business: **Believe in your idea, and be selective about the advice you take.**

Feedback is helpful in refining a business model, especially a business model that is the first of its kind. But the important thing when listening to feedback is to filter it. Yes, it's good to talk to smart, experienced business people about your idea. But—quick tip—it's dangerous to accept feedback from someone who is not giving you at least an hour of undivided attention. I've never met a dumb venture capitalist, but I have had plenty of dumb conversations with them. They have an alien-like compulsion to try to sound intelligent. Many of them believe every good business idea should be explainable in a single sentence, called an elevator pitch. If you don't win their heart in the first ten seconds, they are going to tell you for the next sixty minutes why your business probably won't work. I've never ever had a VC change her mind after her first ten-second impression was formed.

In any event, no matter how many times venture capitalists told me my idea wasn't super-awesome, I got a ton of encouragement and feedback from those who matter more: prospective customers. And I got a lot of support from family and friends who took the time to talk with me, to dig into details, and to help me shape Shopatron into a business.

Eventually, after talking to everyone and hearing both pros and cons, I still could not imagine a world without this solution. Once I was convinced Shopatron had a market and a revenue model, the hard part came—I had to actually start the company.

There is no point hedging the bet. If you have listened to the feedback, if you have enough cash to feed your family, if you can see why no one else has done what you want to do but feel desperate nevertheless to do it yourself—push the chips to the center of the table. It's time to go all in.

EARLY DAYS

Despite our passion for the company, success certainly didn't happen overnight.

It took more than a year (from 2000 to 2001) for the software for Shopatron to be developed. In the meantime Robin and I paid the rent by continuing to sell Norvel engines. But by this time, it was becoming clear things were changing in Russia. Putin was in power and the freedom of businesses was being restrained. Military factories were consolidating and the machine tools used to make our engines were re-tasked to make higher margin military wares. There were no political benefits of exporting consumer goods to the United States. Shipments of our engines were delayed and quality was suffering. The end of the Norvel business, at least in its current form, was near.

The sunset of Norvel was what pushed baby Shopatron out of its nest. I didn't have another way to make money in San Luis Obispo, a small town with limited job opportunities. Robin and I loved where we lived, and so did our kids. I was going to have to get Shopatron moving.

The pressure to get Shopatron off the ground mounted through the spring and early summer of 2001. I took stock of where we were: The business model still looked good. The software was coming together. There was still enough sales activity with Norvel to make it a viable test customer for Shopatron.

Two problems were in my way, though. First, the Internet bubble had just popped. Overfunded companies with no revenues were going broke, and venture capitalists were running for cover. Fundraising would be more difficult, and any money raised would cost me a big chunk of the company.

Second, I didn't have the technological know-how to run a software company. It's one thing to pay an outside firm to build a working prototype of a software system. But I would need a technology person to help me launch Shopatron. I attended a tech-networking event hosted by Aspect Media Studios. Nice guys who made videos and TV commercials, and who were trying to extend their business into new web media, ran Aspect. They had transformed their empty studio and storage warehouse into a nightclub for the evening.

A friend bumped into me at the makeshift bar and said, "Hey, I have the perfect technology guy for your new start-up." Sean Collier was the only person I met that night. Sean had just recently shut down a start-up and he and his wife Tracy were moving to Bakersfield so she could take a job there. He hadn't figured out what he was going to do next, maybe go back to school.

That fateful night changed the course of history for the Collier family, because Sean got the Shopatron bug. He and I met a few more times during subsequent weeks. I loved his ability to conceptualize software solutions. He had the technical skills to maintain and even modify Shopatron's code. He was an entrepreneur at heart, a fearless motorcycle rider, and an earnest dude. And let's not forget: his wife had a steady job.

We hammered out a deal for Sean to join Shopatron. He would commute two hours from Bakersfield a few days a week and stay at my house. If the company got big enough, he and Tracy would move back to San Luis Obispo. Sean would take care of technology. I would be in charge of sales and raising money.

Since our bank balance was in the three-digit range, we needed a cheap place to hang our shingle. Our mutual friends at Aspect offered to give us a two-hundred-square-foot corner of their storage warehouse. They wanted some technology influence to rub off on their new media ventures. We wanted free rent.

Our office came with a cement floor and two walls that were eighteen feet high, made of unpainted gray cement blocks. To form two more walls, we procured a couple of cubicle partitions from a nearby start-up that had just gone broke. The partitions were only five feet high, so to hide the piles of props and tools, we borrowed giant sheets of translucent plastic and connected them to the ceiling rafters with orange handyman clamps. The entrance to the place was a sheet of plastic running all the way to the floor, with a human-sized slit we cut for egress. The plastic walls are all people remember about Shopatron's first office.

Besides the aesthetic benefits (if you squinted your eyes, you could pretend the plastic sheets were expensive translucent glass), our makeshift walls served a practical function: insulation. When California got cold and damp in the winter, we plugged in space heaters. A Monday morning that started out at, say, 58 degrees inside our office could reach upwards of 65 degrees by midday, thanks to the more-than-you-might-expect amount of heat plastic walls retain. Long after taking the warehouse space, someone told me that human hands cannot function with full dexterity at ambient temperatures below 65 degrees.

At least the price was right. Our buddies who ran the video production company let us use the space for free for about a year. We then started chipping in a couple of hundred bucks a month for rent. Maybe we would have been more productive in a nicer space. It's no matter now. Starting out lean made sense to me, and it made sense to Sean. We stayed there, cold hands and all, for three-and-a-half years.

BOOTSTRAPPING

By most measures, Shopatron is a very successful business and it makes a difference in the lives of thousands of people every day. We have more than one thousand top brands using our eCommerce solution in ten countries. We have grown at a double-digit rate every year since we launched in 2001. We have 180 employees. My ownership stake in the business is worth millions of dollars.

At the same time, it has taken me twelve long years to get here. Looking back, I sometimes wonder if I would change the way I financed the start-up.

Is it possible we underinvested in the early days? Should we have raised money right when we launched? Would more capital, more people, and more tools in a better office have helped us grow and create a more valuable business faster?

I made a choice to bootstrap the business, which means I financed most of it myself, and operated it during its early years for minimal expenditure. Why did I do this? The biggest reasons were to retain control and encourage innovation, as I will explain later in this chapter.

How did we get by in the early years? The first $100,000 came from the proceeds of our house sale in Ohio when we moved to California. That went straight to the vendor who actually coded the first version of Shopatron from my flow charts and notes. And for the first three years when I did not make a salary, Robin and I used personal credit cards to pay the bills.

All told, I raised four rounds of equity capital for Shopatron: $40,000 from family and friends in 2002, $250,000 from wealthy individuals in early 2004, $500,000 from professional investors in late 2004, and $6 million from professional investors in 2007.

Fundraising is a major commitment. As a company accumulates shareholders over time, each one needs attention. When the time comes to raise new money, existing shareholders want to know why their ownership percentage will be diluted by new money. If the company is raising money to cover net operating losses, shareholders wonder if the business is performing well. The bigger shareholders, especially if they hold veto rights on new money raised, need to formally agree and then still play nice with the new investors.

Fundraising also takes a lot of time. The $40,000 family-and-friends round was the easiest and took only a few weeks. Four individuals invested $10,000 each so we could continue paying Sean his (meager) salary, and buy a server or two. The process involved having our attorney draw up some simple documents, setting a price, making a few phone calls, and then depositing the checks.

The two financing rounds in 2004 were significantly more involved: each took two months of prep work and then two months of intensive effort to close. The process was the same, but with more bells and whistles: drawing up (longer) documents, setting a (higher) price, making (quite a few) phone calls and in-person presentations, and then depositing (bigger) checks.

The largest round, in 2007, took three months of full-time prep work and six full months to pitch and close the deal. Although this round took twice as long as the others, I got more than ten times as much money, learning that it takes proportionally less time if you raise bigger sums of cash all at once. Or as my father once told me at age sixteen, "It takes just as much effort to sell a battleship as it does to sell a sailboat."

Given the time and energy that goes into fundraising, there has to be a very good reason to do it, as it distracts from other parts of your business.

To me, raising money was always a question of milestones and risk management. Sometimes, a company's constituents (customers, employees, shareholders) are simply at the point emotionally where they need to see the company move forward and hit a milestone. Key employees join a start-up because they want to be a part of dynamic growth. If the business appears to be at a plateau, they start wondering if the dream is still alive. Customers, too, who deploy on a new platform, want to see other new companies adopt the technology to validate it. Raising capital is a way to jump start investment in sales and marketing, for example, which can boost the company quickly up to and beyond a milestone everyone has been waiting for.

In 2004, raising capital for Shopatron was all about reaching two key milestones: making a salary and moving us out of the cold warehouse and into a proper office.

By 2007, though, Shopatron was growing and profitable from quarter to quarter. We were beginning to get some real traction in the market. People started noticing us. I decided to raise money then because Shopatron was no longer a stealth start-up. A proven market would entice new competitors to enter our space, both in the United States and in Europe, where we had no service offering.

I was also worried about getting pushed out of the market by a big, well-funded competitor; it was a good time for Shopatron to build a war chest. So I went out and sold one-third of the company to partners who would be at my side should the going get rough. Better to be safe and raise money proactively.

I should note that if we had faced serious direct competition at any point in our start-up history, it would have been essential to raise a lot of capital early to overwhelm the competition and seize the first mover advantage. Fortunately, this was never an issue as Shopatron's order exchange, our core product offering, had an inherently strong and sustainable competitive advantage and was years ahead of its time.

Through the early years at Shopatron I learned lesson number three about launching a business: **Be frugal, and raise capital only when absolutely necessary for survival.** As long as direct competition is not a problem, there is more money to be made by building the business organically.

By staying away from venture capital in our early years, we avoided interference from investors who wanted fast and easy returns. We didn't know exactly how the order exchange would work from a practical point of view, and bootstrapping was a great way for us to develop an advanced business model on a time scale that felt right for us.

Bootstrapping also forced Sean and me to innovate again and again to deliver value at a low cost. Without money to burn, we found clever ways to save cash. We bought used equipment whenever possible. We ran many of our computers on free Linux operating systems instead of on Windows. We migrated our database to MySQL, a free database, to replace Oracle, which was expensive. We built a culture of capital efficiency, which is not possible at any company into which venture capitalists are pouring hot money.

Bootstrapping also meant that we never found ourselves in a position where the company was burning so much money that we had to bring in new capital to survive. We had freedom to approach fundraising when the time was right for us. We could manage the distraction when I had available time and when we had the most leverage (like after signing a big customer or opening a new industry).

Finally, bootstrapping helped me and all the other early shareholders to maintain a significant ownership stake. In the very early days of Shopatron, I read a book (*High Tech Start Up* by John Nesheim) that analyzed hundreds of startups and determined that the founder typically ends up with about 5 percent of the company after all the investors have gotten their piece of the pie. I understood the realities, but I am a man who doesn't really believe in status quo. I was also a man who was living in the middle of the biggest credit boom in history. I could get easy unsecured credit at low interest rates. Why wouldn't I use some of that to build my business? Any self-respecting entrepreneur would lever up to maximize his equity stake, right?

In hindsight, we now know that banks were lending too much money to Americans in the late 1990s and early 2000s. I was one of them. For a period of roughly three years, I would get approved for any credit card for which I applied. By 2004, I had accumulated $180,000 in credit card debt on no fewer than twenty cards. At the peak, Robin and I would get at least one credit card bill in the mail every single day.

Altogether, Robin and I probably paid $40,000 in interest over three years to credit card companies. It might seem weird, but I knew with absolute certainty then that $40,000 would be a great deal for preserving significant additional ownership of Shopatron. We probably saved one-third of our equity (today about 10 percent of the company) through what I now call "the credit card debt maneuver."

Faced with the very real threat of bankruptcy, Robin and I had a basic escape plan worked out. We would go to Bend, Oregon, or some other small town in the West where life was more affordable and live out the rest of our life with the one treasure we could never lose: our love for each other. We had seen what life was like for people in post–Cold War Russia and that put all of our concerns about money in perspective.

LIFE AND LOVE IN RUSSIA

I got through those early bootstrapping days thanks to my supportive wife and a constitution formed by my life experiences. Not just my younger days growing up in an entrepreneurial family, but also my time living in Russia. Making do with less and watching others do the same would forever shape my outlook on life.

Tête à Tête, a French restaurant on Bolshaya Monetnaya Street in St. Petersburg, Russia, had an unassuming mahogany fascia and a heavy double-door entryway. A handful of small tables were scattered throughout the dark but cozy dining room. Usually, one of the tables was occupied by a fat businessman having lunch with his mistress.

The French onion soup was the best thing on the menu. Sparkling mineral water was one of three beverages served. The other two drink options were (both surprisingly good) Russian champagne and Georgian cognac. The noise and fumes of the Soviet-era automobiles and trucks, rumbling down the street, were held at bay.

In 1992, Vasily Petrovich, a former KGB agent who had been assigned as my escort, brought me to Tête à Tête at lunchtime during my first day working at Pirometer, a military aviation components factory located a half-mile down the road. In fact, he brought me there every day for four months. Although now there are many great places to eat lunch in St. Petersburg, at that time, within walking distance of Pirometer, there was just Tête à Tête.

I was the first American to be on the payroll of a Russian military factory after the Cold War. Pirometer had grim looking security guards, KGB guys lurking around especially secret areas, and rotary phones. The boss had no fewer than six rotary phones on his desk. Vasily, who I learned was a former trainer of Egyptian soldiers and served on the UN mission to Israel, accompanied me wherever I went at the factory, even to the bathroom.

I didn't have a job description. And I didn't really do anything during the day. The head of my department, the foreign relations department, was a relative of a big boss. Nobody seemed to do anything except talk politics. They pretended to pay us, and we pretended to work.

It took me a few months to get fluent speaking Russian, and a few months more to find something interesting to do at work. One day, I got a preview of some spear guns they were making. I asked if the spear guns were being sold abroad. No, they said, and thus my Seabear business (that I described earlier) began. I felt lucky to have such an interesting opportunity, and I didn't think about how much money I would make.

On Thursdays after work, I would go to the Banya, the sauna, with the guys. When a group of Russian men go to a sauna, it's their version of poker night. Except you get nude, drink vodka, jump in the sauna, and have a close buddy give you a face-to-the-bench whipping with birch switches. After you prove your manliness by withstanding unspeakable heat and humidity in the box, you jump into an unheated pool of non-chlorinated water. Grab another shot of vodka and maybe a bite of salami or cheese, or pig's blood if it's a special occasion, and then do it all again.

Occasionally when I would show up to work, there would be a caravan ready: three Volga cars belonging to the head honchos at the factory, and some minivans for supplies. We would drive a few hours, take a shot of vodka here and there, stop for cigarette breaks, and end up in the forest somewhere eating kabobs cooked over fire. One car ride led us to the swampy Estonian border, where we picked mushrooms amidst war relics like pillboxes and trenches.

In any event, after a few weeks of having lunch together every day, Vasily and I got to know each other pretty well. He had perfect English, impeccable manners, and was always fun to be around. He knew that Robin, my girl-friend from California, was coming to St. Petersburg to live with me. He knew that she and I had met on a blind date while at Stanford. He also knew that I had decided, immediately upon Robin's arrival in Russia, to ask her to marry me.

Vasily with great excitement took me to a nearby jewelry store to buy a ring. I didn't shop around—he knew one place that could be trusted to sell real gold with real jewels. I made my choice, paid the portly woman in the cashier booth, and returned to the counter to retrieve my purchase. No jewelry store velvet-covered box—just wrapped in brown paper—the gold, delicate flower-shaped ring with a ruby inset cost me $29.

I took Robin to Tête à Tête the first evening she was in St. Petersburg. Over French onion soup, I clumsily popped the question. She said "Yes!" and we toasted our future with a shot of cognac—they had run out of champagne. Our Russian adventure, an experience we would share for the rest of our lives, had begun.

Our apartment, which took much of our stipend money, was in a new build-ing overlooking the Finnish Gulf. We had no microwave, no dishwasher, no washer or dryer for our clothes, and, worst of all, only three channels to pick from on our television. Santa Barbara, the American soap opera dubbed into Russian, was our favorite show. When expanded for sleeping, our sofa bed would often collapse to the floor due to its unthinkably poor design.

On December 31, we hosted a New Year's party in that apartment. New Year is a big deal in Russia, probably the biggest holiday of the year. Around 1 a.m., well after the New Year cheering was done, Robin and I started giving each other that "when in the hell are our guests to leave" look. We politely inquired with the person we trusted most, Irina, who laughed and told us that the tra-dition in Russia is for New Year's parties to go until daylight. The reason: Few Russians had cars, St. Petersburg is a huge sprawling city, and the Metro closed at midnight. So partying to 6 a.m. was really just a practicality.

Although we had a good spread that night at our party, for the most part Robin and I ate poorly in Russia. In St. Petersburg in 1992, there was no mod-ern grocery store. Buying food was a considerable problem. Sugar was rationed. Eggs could be bought off the back of a truck. It took an hour by subway to get to an open-air market. We were afraid to buy meat.

Living in Russia made it abundantly clear that material wealth was not necessary for happiness. Many of the Russians I knew lived rich, meaningful lives without a lot of material possessions. A typical Russian family in 1992 did not own a car. Meals consisted of potatoes, a little meat, and soup. Travel abroad was impossibly expensive. Clothing and household items were replaced only when functionally required.

Yet the warmth and hospitality felt upon being a guest in a Russian household exceeded anything Robin and I have experienced. A Russian tradition holds that, when a guest enters your home, it's like God entering your home. The number of dishes cooked for the guest represents your level of respect.

Once we had a meal with thirty unique dishes cooked. It must have taken a week of shopping to find all those ingredients and prep those dishes. Another time, in a small Russian village, we were served the very last bit of pork the family had from their slaughtered family pig. (It was a big chunk of multi-layered fat, which I could consume only after a couple shots of moonshine, but it was a gift I cherish to this day.)

When there is no wealth, there is still the miracle of human connection. There are friends, memories, traditions, and laughter. And, most importantly, there is love.

Love is a good thing for an entrepreneur to have in his back pocket, because love is the ultimate risk mitigation strategy. I've been asked a hundred times: how in the world did you deal with the risk of taking on so much credit card debt to launch Shopatron?

It's not complicated. I was certain my wife would love me no matter what happened with Shopatron. I took the risk because I really had nothing valuable to lose—just money.

LAUNCH

On August 18, 2001, Shopatron accepted order number 64587. A man named Hal Dale placed an order on the website of Sullivan Products, a hobby parts manufacturer and the first real client of Shopatron. The order was reviewed online by three retailers, some of our earliest adopters, and was ultimately fulfilled by Hobby Haven in Overland Park, Kansas. It was delivered to Mr. Dale two days later.

Sean and I gave each other a big high five. A retailer had actually logged into Shopatron, found the page where the order was listed, requested the order, and fulfilled it. We didn't have to call the retailer. The automated e-mail that alerted him to an available order had worked, and the retailer had taken the initiative and figured out how to make money through Shopatron.

I think the plastic sheet walls of our office were shaking with excitement.

Over two years in the making, Shopatron's order exchange had functioned as planned. A consumer had shopped at the manufacturer website and placed an order. A nearby retailer who had the product in stock had fulfilled the order.

That month, over seventy orders were fulfilled by retailers participating in our order exchange. Shopatron made $866 in revenue on those orders. It may not seem like a lot of money, but it was more than what we had in our bank account when we started the month. We could afford to replace the laser printer that just died, which meant we could print the check to mail to the retailer to reimburse him for his fulfillment activity.

What I remember most from that first month, though, was this: the profound relief of watching my newfangled business pass test after test after test.

I have always felt that, in the period after an entrepreneur launches his business, he must beware. The temptation to ignore fatal flaws in the business model is lurking, ready to suck him into years of throwing good money after bad, pretending that his idea is viable when really it failed to excite the market. Overconfidence can be the entrepreneur's greatest weakness.

And yet, the entrepreneur must have confidence and conviction because he is, in some ways, absolutely alone. No other human being on earth assembled the pieces of his start-up puzzle. No one else listened to the hundreds of points of feedback, talked to dozens of prospective customers, or spent thousands of hours contemplating how to enter the market.

So if the business is working, he must ignore the naysayers, the venture capitalists, and the prospects who won't return a call. It's time to rally the troops to celebrate the win and to gather spirit for the next advance. It is going to take a lot of energy to build an actual company out of this. Let's get moving.

For, after the launch, comes the hardest part: selling the solution to enough customers to keep the doors open.

CHAPTER TWO
SALES TRAINING

In the Stevens family, it was a tradition to become a furniture salesman at age sixteen. My dad, four uncles, six cousins, and my older brother began their salesman apprenticeships at sixteen. Like the nearby Amish boys who learned how to be carpenters at a young age, we were taught the family business whether we liked it or not. In 1977, my dad opened the Furniture Depot, a retail furniture store in Cuyahoga Falls, Ohio, near Akron. I was nine years old at the time. Through the next ten years, I held a number of jobs at the Depot: dusting boy, stock boy, delivery boy, receptionist, and—at the peak of my career—salesman.

Dressing up, facing stern-faced shoppers, and explaining the benefits of solid oak over veneer does not now, and did not then, inherently sound like fun to a teenager. Talking with adults is torture enough. Talking adults into buying furniture? Never going to happen.

Yet, as you might guess, it did happen, and how it happened is a good lesson in incentives.

My parents had the absolute power to force me to work at their store. But they couldn't force me to be enthusiastic about doing so. And let me tell you, if a sixteen-year-old boy is not enthusiastic when trying to sell something to adults, he might as well pound sand. But my mom and dad were wise and drew from the time-tested Stevens incentive playbook. In exchange for my donning a tie and slogging to work every Saturday and Sunday during the school year and five days a week during the summer, they offered me the one thing I couldn't refuse: a brand new sports car.

My incentive was a shiny blue 1985 Pontiac Trans Am, V8, stick shift, with the premium sound and wheel package. Let me just tell you this was one sweet ride. It was worth every bit of furniture-selling humiliation and rejection to get that car.

But six days after picking up the Trans Am from the dealership, I was racing a friend on a busy highway in downtown Akron. I mis-shifted, skidded, and plowed into a guardrail. My new ride, temporary paper license plate and all, lay crumpled and destroyed. Sirens. Police. Shock.

I can't remember how I got home that day, or what I said to Mom or Dad. I do remember putting my face into my pillow and crying myself to sleep.

The next day, my dad woke me up early and told me to put on a tie and get ready for work. I did not feel like selling furniture, but I thought it better not to mention this. He sat me in the leather driver's seat of his beige Cadillac El Dorado and told me to drive.

As we took the familiar route to work, my dad lectured me. Not about being ungrateful, or careless, or stupid. He was a lot more understanding than I expected. He mentioned that he was glad I was safe. Then he said that, if I sell one extra sofa that day, any bump in insurance premium that might arise from this accident would be covered. Get back on the horse and earn your way out of this situation.

After a few weeks, my mom and dad replaced my blue Trans Am with a black one.

Here's the way I earned it:

Imagine a sixteen-year old zit-faced kid is standing near the front door of a furniture store, watching a middle-aged couple walk in. The kid is dressed earnestly in a white short sleeve, button-down shirt, a navy blue knit tie, khaki pants, and Sperry topsiders. His outfit is designed to show respect or, perhaps, beg for mercy.

The kid says, "Hi, Welcome to the Furniture Depot. Are you looking for anything special today?"

"No, we're just looking."

A typical response. But by now my dad has taught me a couple things about selling. First, men, under any circumstances, do not come into a furniture store to look around for fun. Even women rarely enter a store without some kind of intent to purchase. Time is the most valuable thing people have and they won't waste one minute shopping without a reason.

Second, shoppers tell you they are "just looking" because they don't want to tell *you* what's on their mind. They might say they don't want to be hassled, but the truth is that they are often confused about what they want, how much to spend, etc., and don't think you can help them unravel the confusion. That is why, as Dad has taught me, you have to engage them in conversation; otherwise your chances of making a sale are zero. He tells me he has never, in thirty years, seen a customer walk around the store alone and then just decide to buy a $1,000 sofa.

"Well, that's ok. I'm just showing," I reply.

My response doesn't get a huge smile from the weary couple. I might have even sounded snippy. Damn, I need to work on my tone. It doesn't matter; I've made my point: You are in my store, which is not a free museum for people who like to look at furniture. You can leave if you want, but while you are here I am going to talk to you. I may be young, but I know a lot more about furniture than you do, and I am here to help you.

I try to establish rapport by talking about the weather, the Cleveland Browns, or some of the new items we just received. As we walk around, the couple is looking at the price tags. They are touching fabrics. After a few minutes, they feel safe enough to tell me they are looking for a new sofa for their family room. Bingo.

"Something for a new room? A replacement?" I need to know where they are coming from. What did they not like about their old sofa. Wore out too quickly? Fabric got too dirty? Not comfortable? Negative associations are most likely to drive their decision this time around.

As the discussion continues, it becomes clear this couple is serious about buying. Even better, they seem to be attracted to the brown velour motion sofa with two recliners built in. The one with the beer can cooler and telephone in the armrest. Not one of my dad's better purchasing decisions. We've been trying to sell this contraption for more than a year.

In the furniture business, a slow moving sofa is called a "dog" because it just lies around on the floor and rarely moves. After spending some time with the dog, you get to know it, speculating about what it needs. It's a bit shallow on the seat—maybe a short guy will buy it. Yeah, let's pair it with some bigger lamps, maybe move it by the window where there is better light. But nothing helps. It just sits there. For months. And months. People don't want to buy this sofa.

There was no act bestowing greater prestige on a member of the Depot's sales force than selling a dog, and that is what I did that day. Dad watched through the office window as I sat at the table with the customers, writing up the sale. Never tell jokes when writing up a sale, Dad taught me. It's a serious thing for someone to spend $1,000. Get the payment right. Cash or check is always better than credit cards. Give the customers their copy of the paperwork and thank them for their business.

After the customers are gone, Dad gave me a big smile and a pat on the back. I pulled off one the greatest magic tricks in the business. I turned a dog into $1,000 cash.

Looking back, the most important thing I learned as a teenage salesman at the Furniture Depot was how to handle rejection. I developed a leathery exterior that could weather the constant flow of negative customer comments. Too expensive. Too plain. Too big. Too small. I learned to stand tall when a customer said no or stared at me in steely silence. I focused on the one response that mattered—"I'll take it." Making a sale felt better than getting an "A" on a calculus test. One happy customer gave me a rush that wiped away the memories of many others who did not buy.

I learned a few other important lessons as well. Open and honest discussion with customers leads to better results, and you have to work hard to build trust. Taking care of people—both customers and suppliers—pays off when times get tough. If a customer walks in the door five minutes before closing time, stay as late as necessary to serve them; a customer rarely comes back once they leave.

My teenage salesman experience, and all the lessons I took away from it, were invaluable when it came time, fifteen years later, to sell eCommerce solutions for Shopatron.

SELLING A VISION

Turn the clock to 2003.

I have bet my life savings on Shopatron, an Internet start-up, even though I have zero experience in making or selling software and dotcoms have been failing right and left. I've found a partner to help me launch the company. He's in charge of technology and operations, and I'm in charge of sales and marketing.

My job is to convince real customers to pay actual money to use our new eCommerce solution. How will I do this?

Over the years I have read dozens of books on selling techniques: *Zig Ziglar's Secrets of Closing the Sale, Strategic Selling, How to Be a Rainmaker, Selling to VITO*, and more. I have taken a Miller Heiman sales training course. Investing time in being a more effective salesperson has always paid off for me. Every time I read a sales book, I picked up at least one or two valuable tips.

The fundamentals of selling are usually the same no matter the industry: Ask a lot of questions. Don't talk over customers (they don't care how smart you are). Sell benefits, not features. Find out directly what concerns are holding the customer back from buying. Be enthusiastic, because customers make decisions based on emotion.

However, I soon discover that these mainstream sales books and trainings offer precious little wisdom to a bootstrapping entrepreneur selling a radical new idea to businesses. Since at this point Shopatron has raised little or no capital from investors, there is no marketing budget to pay for shiny brochures, slick websites, or Super Bowl commercials. When I meet with potential customers, it's just me and my business cards.

The bootstrapped start-up salesman begins each sales cycle with a deep deficit of credibility. Through experimentation and luck, I develop five techniques that build credibility and establish Shopatron as a solution worth serious consideration.

5. Be serious.

Just as my dad taught me, there is nothing to be gained by acting jocular with customers. They are taking a chance with a start-up solution. This is not playtime.

Being serious is not the same thing as pretending to be a big company. It means demonstrating that you know you are going to be a big company someday. Act like the president of the United States. Do not get drunk in public. Do not go to strip bars with prospective customers. Do not tell off-color jokes or slap anyone's back. It may be effective for the typical salesman to do these things, but not for a CEO who sells. You want customers to think you are wound a bit too tight, so they feel comfortable placing their business in the hands of a responsible nerd.

4. Never acknowledge that your business model could be flawed in any way. Ever.

A visionary does not debate his vision. While diplomatic argument requires acknowledgment of the other person's point of view, you cannot bet your life savings on an idea and then openly discuss the possibility that the idea might not be valid. If a prospective customer, no matter how big or important he may be, is challenging your business model, you must stare at him with knowing eyes. Always exude confidence that you are ahead of the game.

I always found it useful to say, "Well, of course, not every company is going to use my solution, but those that want to grow their sales with retailers will use it." Do not give in. Everyone is testing to see if you are true to your vision.

3. Go guerrilla.

Do whatever it takes to stand out. Nothing matters if you don't get noticed. Creative marketing and sales approaches, as long as they are not silly, resonate well when trying to sell a new, creative way of doing business. The book *Guerrilla Marketing* by Jay Conrad Levinson is a great source of inspiration.

As an example, when I was trying to break into the quilt and sewing market for Shopatron, I wore a quilted tie to the trade shows. Every woman in every booth asked me, "Where did you get that tie?" I replied, "My mom made it for me." Boom. I'm in.

2. Build credibility without references.

You will not have any customers to reference when you sell your first customer, and you will not have any big customers to reference when you try to sell your first big customer. What are some ways I found to get around this?

First, deploy a money-back guarantee. This is the mother of all credibility-building sales techniques, used by countless infomercials: "No, as a matter of fact, I do not have any customers your size. But if you are concerned if Shopatron will work for you, I understand. That's why we offer a one-hundred-day money-back guarantee."

Second, locate your start-up in a place where it will be associated with bigger companies. Investment firm? Locate on Wall Street or its local equivalent. Tech company? No location is better known than California. When prospects would ask me where we were located, I'd say California. And they would say, "Yeah, that's where all those new Internet companies come from."

Third, overdress. At the outdoor sporting goods show, most exhibitors (my prospects) wore casual hiking clothes. I wore a coat and tie. They probably thought I was a geek but, then again, that's what I wanted them to think—I will take care of all that software stuff. And every once in a while, I would bump into an old school exec wearing a coat and tie. Those types love young guys in suits.

1. Show how you will ease the customer's pain.

This is by far the most critical sales technique for bootstrapping start-ups.

If a new solution is going to make it in the real world, and if customers are going to take a chance with a brand new company selling it, there had better be some real need for the solution in the first place.

Human beings being wired the way they are, they spend most of their money on solutions that eliminate some kind of problem, or pain, which they experience on a regular basis (it's why, for example, they hire accountants or payroll services). Businesses don't spend money; people inside businesses spend money. And those people don't like pain. They will do crazy things to avoid it.

When selling Shopatron solutions in the early days, I certainly had my fair share of credibility obstacles to overcome. First, we had to get customers comfortable with the fact that we would be handling the financial transactions. That Shopatron, a tiny new start-up, would store the consumer's personal and credit card information and would take the customers money and keep it for a week or two before paying to the retailer that ships the consumer's order.

Second, we were going to do this with no track record in the eCommerce industry, no recognizable customers, and, course, no carpet or heat in our office. There were a lot of reasons not to do business with us.

The one thing we did have going for us was *pain*. Not our pain—our prospective customers' pain.

That's the good kind of pain. You can't have a start-up without it. Pain is what gets an otherwise rational buyer, a buyer who knows better, to take a chance with an unproven start-up located in a warehouse.

To our prospective customers, manufacturers of consumer products, the boom in Internet sales was actually painful. They wanted to take their sales online and reap the benefits of this new sales channel, but they knew over the long run it was foolish to compete directly with their own customers (retailers who would see their sales undercut). And even when manufacturers did try to sell to consumers, they typically did it poorly by not listing all their products or by jacking up the prices so that retailers wouldn't get upset.

Believe me, every single manufacturer in the world was feeling this pain. And Shopatron was there to ease it. But first I had to get those initial customers on board.

CHICKEN OR EGG

Selling Shopatron's solution in the early days was a labor of love that tested 100 percent of my sales seasoning. I had no money to spend on advertising or marketing. I did have a computer and a telephone.

The first two companies to launch on Shopatron were through my hobby industry connections: Norvel, my own model engine company, and Lite Machines, a maker of model helicopters. I brought the president of Lite Machines, Paul Arlton, on board as a founder of Shopatron, giving him four hundred thousand shares, a considerable sum.

The first real, non-affiliated customer for Shopatron, Sullivan Products, was owned by Jim Hudson, an engaging and friendly man who made parts and accessories for radio control airplanes in an immense, turn-of-the-century era factory in downtown Baltimore. We would need many more customers like Sullivan to get rolling.

It was the late summer of 2002 and the big annual hobby trade show in Chicago was coming up. I went to the trade show website, found the exhibitor listing, and called each and every exhibitor in the months ahead of the show. Many hung up on me or denied me the opportunity to discuss the wonderful benefits of retail-integrated eCommerce. But it was important for Sean to hear me selling, and heaven knows we needed the leads, so I made up a game where I couldn't stop working for the day until I had five quality conversations with prospects.

I flew to Chicago and got a badge from Paul to get into the show. I walked around from booth to booth and talked to anyone who would listen, developing a sense for when a person was open to conversation. Fortunately, most of the people I spoke to felt the pain. They were ready to listen to me.

My pitch sounded like this:

Every day people visit your website. If they can't buy the product there, some of these customers will go to online retailers or even to a local store to buy the product they find at your site. But many of them will get distracted along the way. They will find your competitor's product. They will lose the emotional impulse to buy. Anything can happen once the customer has left your website, and most of these things do not involve buying your product.

Instead of letting these customers leave your site, give them the opportunity to buy without friction. Put up a Shopatron-powered eCommerce store and list your entire range of products. Customers will visit the store and buy products at your site.

Your retailers will not be angry with you, because Shopatron enables you to partner with your retailers as order fulfillment partners for your eCommerce program.

To place an order, a customer simply shops in the store, puts items in their shopping cart, and checks out as in any online shopping site. They enter their name, address, and payment information. Shopatron receives this information into its servers.

Immediately, the order is placed into the Shopatron order exchange. Think of the order exchange as a bucket, a bucket that holds consumer orders.

Retailers who sign up for free with Shopatron are given access to look in the bucket to see the orders customers are placing. Retailers can place a flag on an order to request it. The order is not assigned to the first retailer who puts a flag on it. Every retailer in the system is given a fair chance to see orders and request orders.

At 1:30 p.m. Eastern time, Shopatron's computers look at the orders in the bucket and pick the closest stocking retailer who has requested the order.

The great thing about Shopatron is that orders from other manufacturers in your industry are also in the bucket. So the retailers like coming to Shopatron to see what is selling from all participating manufacturers and to make sales from all of them as well.

Typically, an interested prospect would ask dozens of questions on how the model worked. I would answer them patiently, proving that we had thought of all the angles and that Shopatron was an intelligent and viable solution.

Then I would get the hardest questions:

How many retailers do you have participating? Which manufacturers?

At this point, there were just three manufacturers using Shopatron and maybe ten retailers. Not an impressive tally. Our first three manufacturers, Norvel, Lite Machines, and Sullivan Products produced only about ten orders a day. Even at the rate of filling one order a week, this would permit only seventy retailers to be on Shopatron and make a sale once a week.

How would it be possible to get manufacturers to sign up without enough retailers already signed up to Shopatron? And how would we get retailers to sign up without enough manufacturers generating orders in the system?

It was a classic chicken or egg problem.

Some manufacturers understood that they would have to bring the retailers to Shopatron. But these innovative, early adopting manufacturers often wanted to know why they were paying an implementation fee to set up Shopatron. They wanted preferential financial terms because they were the first to launch us into their industry. And some of them wanted exclusive access to Shopatron.

I read whatever I could find on solving chicken or egg business development problems. I studied how Visa in its early days (called Bank Americard) spent $100 million convincing merchants to accept credit cards even though few consumers carried credit cards. I read how Microsoft primed the market and lost money on every Xbox sold in order to assure video game developers there would be a big market for Xbox games. This in turn assured Microsoft there would be lots of royalties from games sold.

Nothing I read was really applicable, but experimentation over time revealed how Shopatron could build its two-sided marketplace. Free implementation never brought in any customers. In fact, manufacturers were happy to pay a little up front to get better service when launching an important strategic program.

Exclusives for early adopters gave us some limited success, but the exclusives that lasted more than a year distorted the order exchange and ultimately led to poor results for clients. Going back to my sales training at the Furniture Depot, though, I knew a sale is made when the customer believes they need the benefit of your product. Good old-fashioned selling of benefits, that is, explaining to each customer how our solution would ease their pain, worked better than any fancy tricks.

During the six years when I was the sales lead for Shopatron, I pitched thousands of manufacturers on the benefits of selling online and partnering with retailers as order fulfillment partners. Most of my selling was done by phone. There is no selling method more cost effective or time efficient than phone sales. I could prospect in high volume and have five or so good "meetings" a single day.

Even if I am trying to sell them on the unfortunate day when our landlord, the video production company fifteen feet away from our office, decides to use their studio.

Prospective customers are more like cats than dogs. They are elusive. They don't sit and roll over, and they certainly don't come when called. If I got a long awaited e-mail from a prospect who (finally) is ready to talk to me about his pain, I am that prospect's bitch. If that e-mail says "call me at 11 a.m.," that is now the most important time of the day. Everything—eating, drinking, peeing—must conform to the moment of time when the prospect wants to talk about his pain.

Even when, at that same time, a group of twenty actors, cameramen, and technicians start shooting a commercial just on the other side of our plastic-sheet wall.

I knew that our landlord would be angry if I picked up the phone and talked to my prospect. I would disrupt their filming and cost them money and time by forcing a retake.

At that point, though, it was killed or be killed. I would rather be evicted than lose the one prospect this week who wants to talk to me about his pain. Nothing was more important than talking to my prospect when she opened the door for me to talk with her.

———

One of my favorite tactics for getting in front of people who refused to take my phone calls was to attend a trade show. In 2005 and 2006, I attended more than sixty trade shows. It was lonely but effective work.

Each trade show day began at 6 a.m. with a fill-me-up-for-the-day breakfast. (Eating lunch would be a waste of available selling time.) I would arrive at an expo center at 7 a.m. It would take at least an hour to plot my "must visit" list on the trade show map. I could make fifteen meetings in a day only if my walking course through the show was time efficient.

At that point, I would do what every self-respecting entrepreneur would do: try to get onto the show floor early (I tried each entrance until I found a security guard that would let me in). Catch a bigwig executive before her first meeting began, while she was fresh, and I would have a higher chance of getting her to listen to a new idea. Also, since only exhibitors were allowed on the floor before the show opened, if I were on the floor early, it made me look more like an insider.

No one could accuse me of getting lucky with the successful launch of Shopatron. I carried the company on my back for six years, from trade show to trade show, talking to anyone who would listen. Relentless repetition of my sales pitch. Exhausted legs, back, and shoulders. I still have a strawberry-size bone spur on the top of my left shoulder where, day after day, a leather strap held my fifteen-pound computer-laden briefcase.

In January 2006, I endured a four-show, eleven working-days-in-a-row tour. I started in Vegas at the Hunting show (three days) and then hit the Ski show (three days). I flew to Salt Lake City to cover the Winter Outdoor show (three days). Then I flew back to Vegas to hit the Vacuum and Sewing show (two days). Each evening, I would retire to my hotel room, pull off my damp leather shoes, and collapse on the bed. Five or six hours of sleep later, I'd be dragging myself out of bed for another day of selling.

It took every ounce of my mental energy to walk up to yet another booth, put on a brave smile, and engage a prospective customer who most likely will not buy. In the course of those eleven days, I spoke with more than 300 people about Shopatron. Of those, 295 of them declined to do business with us.

For a salesman, rejection is a head wind that never stops blowing. Sometimes it's an annoyance that only slows you down while you still make steady progress. Other times, it's a hurricane so strong you feel lucky to lean forward and just stand still against it.

The best inspiration to keep moving forward was, without a question, the memories of past sales made. I kept my storage banks full of client acquisition tales, which I would tell to myself and to Sean whenever we needed a boost.

One by one, I brought new manufacturers onto the Shopatron network. We ended up with hundreds of great companies using Shopatron by March 2007, when I finally handed the sales reins over to Brian Clausen. But, of course, we had our share of setbacks along the way.

SETBACKS

Our first big customer in the hobby industry was Sig Manufacturing. Located in a soybean field outpost called Montezuma, Iowa, Sig was owned by a hard-drinking New Zealander named Chris Le Heron. Chris had bought the company from Hazel Sig, a motorcycle-riding, aerobatic plane–flying wonder woman. Sig made wooden model airplane kits, engine fuel, and accessories. The management team at Sig, a genuine group of guys, partied more than any professional men or women I have ever encountered.

There really was only one way to earn Chris' trust and Sig's business; I had to break my sales rule #5 and drink right along with them. Business dinners began with at least two happy hour cocktails. A hearty steak dinner was washed down with a couple bottles of red wine. Every meal ended with a liqueur, and then we would hit the bar—any bar—and after last call we would hit the Jim Beam in somebody's kitchen. The ordeal would end around two or three in the morning at the earliest, and put the drinking I'd done with the Russians to shame.

When I say I experimented on how to solve the chicken or egg problem, I mean it. I had to do anything to build relationships and get my first customers. Including becoming an alcoholic for a week at a time while visiting the guys from Sig and attending model airplane fly-ins. So when Sig called us up a year or so after deploying our solution and told us they were going to cancel Shopatron, it hit me hard.

Generally I found that there are two kinds of setbacks in an entrepreneur's world. Of course, there are the big, ugly, company-threatening setbacks: Having a big customer cancel. Having a potential investment deal fall through. Facing a major system outage. Those hurt. But in a way, the big ones are sometimes easier to deal with, because they bring clarity. In the context of a major event, it is easier to understand what went wrong and what must be fixed. In the case of Sig canceling Shopatron, it was clear to me that we needed to increase our efforts building business outside the hobby industry. This "big" customer was unable to integrate online shopping into their website effectively—they were just too small to execute properly. We needed to seek much bigger customers in order to be successful, and we needed to move into bigger industries to find them.

The other kind of setback is more insidious and more demoralizing: the offhand comment from someone close to you, or someone valuable to the business. These subtle yet hurtful comments test you because they cause you to question yourself and your judgment, leaving you wondering if you are on the right course.

Offhand comments I might hear at home:

- Honey, just remember, we always have our backup plan to move to Oregon.
- Dad, why can't we go to Hawaii like Kendra's family?
- So you want me to get a cash advance on our Capital One Visa card and use it to make the monthly payment on our Bank One Visa card?

Or at work:

- Did I hear correctly that our biggest customer might cancel?
- When do you think we are going to make our next sale? It's been a couple months with no sales, right?
- You're a really good salesman, but we aren't going to move forward right now. (Ouch!)

And, of course, those best at damning with faint praise, venture capitalists:

- Shopatron is going to be a great small business.
- eCommerce is an interesting space—I've seen a lot of companies like yours.

One of the most memorable setbacks in Shopatron history involved one of the most prominent venture capital firms in the world.

In early 2006, out of the blue, I got a call from Mark Kvamme, a partner at Sequoia Capital, a venture firm in Silicon Valley famous for investing in Yahoo, Google, Zappos, and LinkedIn. Mark and I talked on the phone for an hour or so, and he was sufficiently interested to fly down and see little Shopatron. I picked him up at the San Luis Jet center, where he landed in his private jet. That was impressive.

Sean and I met with Mark for a couple hours. Then I went to Menlo Park to meet Sequoia's eCommerce committee, including Mike Moritz, maybe the greatest venture capitalist who ever lived.

The committee must have been satisfied, because Mark invited me to come back and pitch all of the partners. I had prepared the best PowerPoint presentation I could while still meeting my goal of pitching five customers a day.

When the partners shuffled in to the conference room, it was clear some of them were going to be more engaged than others. A few of them were eating their breakfast and making small talk. This was a room full of people who could change my life. I had heard that you can tell how interested venture capitalists are in you by how much time they spend with you. Thirty minutes? Forget about it. Two hours? You are likely to get an offer.

The partners spent about an hour and a half grilling me about Shopatron. A week or so later, Mark sent me a term sheet. Unfortunately, the terms were not acceptable. The valuation was fine. But they wanted two out of three board seats. That meant Sequoia would effectively control the company.

My spidey senses were tingling. Every interaction had felt like a Hollywood power game with no attempt to connect with me as a real person. They might as well have pointed a laser gun at me and in a droning voice said, "We are here to take over your planet."

If I had a better vibe about the whole thing, and if the term sheet had been just a little more reasonable, I might just have taken the chance and dived in with this powerful firm. Even if they replaced me as CEO, I would probably make a lot of money while getting some great experience.

But that wasn't the situation. I did the only thing possible: push back on the terms.

There was no response to my counteroffer. Sequoia Capital must not have loved the Shopatron investment opportunity. I had played my cards and lost.

Sean and I were both really disappointed by this outcome. We had not been looking to raise money when Mark first reached out. We went out of our way to talk to this firm, and we ended up wasting a lot of time and emotional energy.

As with most setbacks, we took a minute or two to mourn the situation, and then put our heads down and kept working. Fortunately a breakthrough deal was around the corner.

A BIG WIN

In February 2004, I was at the Toy Fair in New York City. More than one thousand exhibitors displayed their puzzles, stuffed animals, crafts, games, and gizmos in a huge 760,000-square-foot building called Javits Center. Inside was a feast for children's eyes: bright colored booths in every direction displaying fun and fabulous playthings. The warm atmosphere was quite a contrast against the grey and unwelcoming cold outside.

I started my day at the booth of Do-a-Dot, a successful maker of no-mess paints for kids and Shopatron's first client in the toy industry. I said hello to the friendly owners, Rob and Tina, and stashed my winter coat before jumping into battle.

At one point in the morning, I walked by a big white booth covered in primary yellow, blue, and red polka dots. It was packed with salesmen talking to toy store buyers from around the world—clearly a high visibility manufacturer. Above the crowd was a logo hanging from the ceiling. It said Alex Toys.

Like a cat scanning a backyard garden for opportunities, I circled the booth. A group of men in business suits were standing on the aisle. From their body positioning, it looked like the handsome guy in the middle was the alpha male. I can't say how I knew this. I just could tell.

Walking casually into the booth, I started looking at products and touching a couple of them. Avoiding eye contact, I read the alpha male's badge: Rick Amdur.

Then I noted a well-dressed, confident woman showcasing products to three buyers. A quick read of her badge: Nurit Amdur. A husband and wife team.

I walked back over to the area of the booth where the alpha male and his pack were standing. I stood in their line of sight and started inspecting the nearest product in detail, reading the package on all sides, like an expert toy designer. I wanted to appear as though I just might be thinking about copying this product.

I put the toy down and made eye contact with Mr. Amdur. He had been watching me.

"Hello, can I help you with something?" he said.

And that opening was all I needed to launch into my pitch for Shopatron.

After a few minutes of talking, Rick told me that his wife, Nurit, was really in charge of new projects and ideas at Alex Toys. He also told me she was the

CEO and founder. I waited for twenty minutes at least, but Nurit did not become available.

I walked by their booth many more times that day, but she was always busy talking with someone else.

After the show, I followed up with Nurit. Much to my surprise, she took my phone call on my very first attempt. That's really unusual for a CEO.

"Thank you for taking my call, Nurit," I said.

"It's no problem. I take every call, because I never know where the next innovative idea is going to come from," she replied.

I went on to pitch her on Shopatron. She understood the concept. Selling online would open a new channel for consumers on the Alex Toys website. And give her sales team new partnership opportunities with retailers.

A few weeks later, the signed contract rolled through the fax machine. It was the biggest client win in Shopatron history.

That night, Sean and I celebrated at Bull's Tavern, a famous dive bar in downtown San Luis Obispo. Celebrating victories is crucial to maintaining high morale for a start-up company. Each success story, the more it is told, becomes etched in the memories of founders and employees alike. There are many challenges a start-up faces on its path to success. It's important to store up every bit of positive energy and save it for a rainy day.

The positive vibes of a big customer acquisition also serve as notice to each and every person inside a start-up. The company has made it to a higher level; its leaders need to raise their game, too. As Shopatron continued to grow, my role was evolving from a one-man sales band into that of a CEO leading a global eCommerce company. To manage a business that would work with thousands of customers, I would have to raise my leadership game, drawing yet again on past experiences.

CHAPTER THREE
A LESSON IN HUMILITY

I n 1987, the United States Naval Academy was the most selective college in America. More than fifteen thousand young men and women competed for just twelve hundred appointments.

I had been inspired to apply by Maverick and Goose. So had many others: the Class of 1991 was called the Top Gun class because applications surged after the hit movie glamorized the life of a naval aviator.

The admissions process was intense and went beyond the typical college application, essays and standardized tests. There was a physical fitness test: how many push-ups, sit-ups, and pull-ups could I do in a minute, plus agility work. The medical exam required the doctor to wear rubber gloves and me to bend over. Local alumni interviewed me for character and leadership potential. My local US congressman met with me and asked me why I should be the individual who would get his single slot in the upcoming class.

Despite my best efforts and solid test scores, I was nevertheless rejected for admission. In March of 1987, I received a letter in the mail saying "Congratulations, you made it to the final two thousand applicants, but we don't have a congressional nomination available for you this year."

My backup school was Notre Dame, where my brother Cliff was a junior. I forgot about my navy dream and sent them my deposit. On June 9, the pamphlet at my high school graduation read, next to my name, Notre Dame. I still have a copy of it.

On June 15, one week later, I was lounging on the couch at home when the phone rang.

"Ed Stevens?"

"Yes."

"This is Congressman Ed Feighan's office. I want to let you know that a spot has opened up at the Naval Academy for this year. As you know, school starts on July 1. Do you still want a spot?"

Next thing I knew, I was standing on the manicured grounds of the academy. The quaint city center harbor of Annapolis, Maryland, was a few hundred yards behind me. A new adventure was ahead. Armed marines at the gate watched me and hundreds of other young men and women stream towards Halsey Field House, a gymnasium with a copper roof rounded like a aircraft hangar.

We were the Class of 1991, beginning a four-year adventure as midshipmen. If we were fortunate enough to make it through the challenging curriculum and graduate, we would be awarded the privilege of serving five more years in the navy as commissioned officers.

The Naval Academy was founded in 1845 by secretary of the navy, George Bancroft. Its graduates include countless heroes and notable leaders. Nimitz. Perot. Carter. McCain.

Even though I had barely squeaked in, I felt damn good about myself on that fine July morning. My grade point average in high school had been just a shade under 4.0. I had been a two-way starter on a top-twenty division I football team. I was a hard-working salesman at my parents' furniture store. Teachers gave me positive recommendations.

I did well. I deserved to be there. And I didn't think there was anything wrong with feeling that way. Self-confidence is not a bad trait in a sailor or a soldier. It takes a backbone to land a jet on an aircraft carrier, to drive a ship in fifty-foot seas, or for that matter, to kill another human being in combat.

So I had self-confidence, but did I have that most admired quality in leaders: courage? What makes a person courageous is not simply an abundance of confidence. It's humility.

Humility comes from knowing failure. It comes from knowing fear, pain, and grief so well that you are not afraid to face any of them again. That is what the Naval Academy sought to teach us. **That what makes a good leader is humility**.

"We must always provide the Naval service with leaders who demonstrate excellence in carrying out all their duties, but who do so with humility—achieving excellence without arrogance," says the welcome message on the Naval Academy website.

My plebe year indoctrination was certainly a humbling experience. After getting my head shaved and changing into a pure white cotton sailor suit, I said goodbye to my parents and hello to hell.

I walked into Bancroft Hall, a complex of buildings in which all midshipmen lived. I had been given instructions to meet up with my new company mates and assemble in our corridor. There was Jim from Nashville, Irene from Montana, and Adam from Arizona. Shiny blue floor tiles squeaked as we and about thirty other plebes of twentieth company lined up against the green square concrete walls.

The first thing we learned when the lights went out and the hazing began were the acceptable responses of a plebe. Except for giving specific information requested by an upperclassman, we were allowed to give just one of five responses to any question:

Yes, sir. No, sir. Aye, aye, sir. No excuse, sir. I'll find out, sir.

"Yes, sir" and "No, sir" are self-explanatory. "Aye, aye, sir" is used to acknowledge a direct command.

"Stevens, go down to the storage room and get a mop. Hold it high above your head as you bring it back here. This floor is damn disgusting. You're going to clean it until it shines like the paint on a brand new Camaro. Well don't just look at me. Get moving!"

"Aye, aye, sir."

The other two responses, "No excuse, sir," and "I'll find out, sir," which I learned in the first five minutes of hazing, are fundamental and powerful.

Let's say my classmate John Meyer and I are standing next to each other, sweating profusely thanks to the hot Maryland summer, our backs against the concrete wall. Mr. Cherry, a slender, erudite, and surprisingly sinister upperclassman in charge of hazing us, asks:

"Mr. Meyer, what is the maximum speed of an F-14 Tomcat?"

Unfortunately John does not know the answer. A wrestling champion from Iowa, John is a stud whom anyone would want on their side of a firefight in Afghanistan. But memorization is not his forte.

He has only one answer available at this point:

"I'll find out, sir."

At the Naval Academy, you could never say "I don't know" or "I'm not sure" or "I could take a guess." You either knew the answer, or you made yourself accountable for finding out the answer.

Imagine just for a minute what it would be like if everyone in the world said "I'll find out" when they didn't know an answer.

"Susan, can you tell me which of our top one hundred customers are going to be at the trade show on Tuesday night?"

"I'll find out, sir!"

"John, what is the statistical likelihood of a meteor hitting the two of us standing here on a street corner in San Luis Obispo, California?"

"I'll find out, sir!"

The Naval Academy is this kind of world. Each and every midshipman could depend on his classmate to be accountable for figuring out what needed to be figured out. The buck always stopped. You do your job, and I'll do mine. It was a unique and powerful bond among peers.

Apparently, though, being part of a great culture of accountability did not effuse any sense of serenity on Mr. Cherry. Facing us from just twelve inches, eyeballs bulging bigger, the seething Mr. Cherry turns his attention to me and asks the same question.

"Well, what about you, Mr. Stevens? What is the maximum speed of an F-14 Tomcat?"

In this case, I know the answer is Mach 2.34, or 1,544 miles per hour.

But I cannot bilge my classmate. The only thing worse than not knowing the answer is knowing the answer and making your classmate look bad.

The US Navy teaches you early that you never leave a member of your team behind. You take care of your platoon, your shipmates, no matter what the consequences are on you. This extends all the way to combat, where the men and women of the navy and marines put themselves in mortal danger just to retrieve the dead bodies of fallen comrades. I pretend I don't know the answer.

"I'll find out, sir."

"You mean you don't know either, Mr. Stevens? That is pathetic. I told you three times to make sure you knew the maximum speed of an F-14. Why don't you know it?"

38

"No excuse, sir."

That is the second powerful phrase. No excuse. There is never an excuse for not knowing something.

This concept of "no excuse" stayed with me and became part of my business ethic. At Shopatron, I am not interested in knowing why you didn't send the client proposal on time. Maybe you are telling me the whole story when you say that your car broke down and your dog died, and maybe you were just being lazy last night and fell asleep watching Monday Night Football. I don't have time to gather evidence and weigh your testimony. You are either unlucky or incompetent. Neither works for me.

"No, c'mon, Mr. Stevens, I really want to know why you don't know. Did you have some big calculus test this morning?"

"No, sir."

"Did you decide it wasn't important and just blew me off?"

"No, sir."

"Then why don't you know it?"

"No excuse, sir."

I look in Mr. Cherry's eyes, and I know that he knows that I know the answer. He doesn't really want to punish me, but he figures the only way to get through to Meyer is to make me pay.

"You really disappoint me, Stevens. I'll tell you what. You can come to my door every day at nineteen hundred hours for the next five days and stand there for five minutes, reciting the maximum speed of the F-14, E-2, Tomahawk missile, Aegis class cruiser, and A-6. Repeat over and over until 19:05 hours. Got that?"

"Aye, aye, sir."

Great. Add "waste five minutes reciting military stats in front of Mr. Cherry's door" to my list of things to do.

In addition to the performance stats of military equipment, plebes also had to memorize (every day) the number of days to graduation; the number of days to the ring dance; the number of days to the next Army/Navy competition; the number of days to the Army/Navy football game; the starting offensive and defensive lineups of the Navy football team and of that week's opponent; individual statistics for the opponent's best players; results of any Army/Navy competitions that took place in the previous week; the complete menu for the next two meals; conversational knowledge of two front page articles and two sporting page articles of the *Washington Post*; the chain of command of the navy; the Mission of the Navy; the flags and symbols for Morse code; and more.

Military training included daily formations, uniform inspections, parade competitions, and, my favorite, room inspections. Room inspectors bounced a quarter on your bed to make sure it was "tight enough." The shower had to be so clean that a black sock rubbed around would not yield the slightest smudge of white soap scum. Floors would need to shine like glass, and dust—well let's just say there wasn't going to be any dust.

As plebes, from the hours of 8 a.m. to 7 p.m., we were required to run, never walk, in the corridors of our dormitory, Bancroft Hall. We had to run in the middle of the hallway, knees high, and could change direction only ninety degrees at a time. If we were to ascend a staircase, we had to run up the outside wall of the staircase, turn ninety degrees at the landing, run to the end of the landing, turn ninety degrees again to go up the next set of stairs, then turn ninety degrees again and again, only to get to the next set of stairs.

In order reach my fifth-floor room from the nearest doorway, I had to make thirty 90-degree turns and run up six flights of stairs.

To make passing through Bancroft Hall even more entertaining for the upperclass, it was mandatory for plebes to shout—loudly—either "Go Navy, sir" or "Beat Army, sir" when making each 90-degree turn. I must have yelled, "Go, Navy, sir" and "Beat, Army, sir" thousands of times in my first year at the academy. To avoid hazing, it was a good idea to yell loudly and keep the chin well braced, turning crisply. Appearing compliant was the best way to avoid an upperclassman still miffed about flunking a test in his high-level electrical engineering class.

All midshipmen ate family-style lunch and dinners seated together in King Hall, its three wings filled with hundreds of heavy wooden tables. Meals were not fun for a plebe. When eating, we were required to move our fork in straight lines, making only ninety-degree movements. Lift the meatball straight up from the plate until it is level with the mouth. Move the meatball horizontally into the mouth. Push the fork horizontally away from the mouth until it is above the next meatball. Lower the fork. Make sure to chew the meatball at least ten times. Sit up perfectly straight and keep your chin braced tightly against your neck.

Throughout each meal, the second class would haze the plebes. They would ask question after question until they found the breaking point, beyond which it was impossible to have memorized the required material. Then they would yell.

There was no way to beat this system.

We had daily physical training, including afternoon sports—I played on the rugby team. Every midshipman was expected to keep himself or herself in great shape and they would time us running a mile or count how many sit ups we could do.

On top of all this, plebes took a full course load at one of the most academically challenging colleges in the world. I took Differential Equations, Chemistry, Computer Programming, English, History, Leadership, and Navigation.

On a typical Tuesday evening at 10 p.m., it was common to face a dilemma like this: should I wax my floor for tomorrow's room inspection, study for my chemistry exam, or memorize the performance characteristics of the Aegis-class cruiser? Something would have to be left undone. I needed at least four or five hours of sleep, after all.

Plebe year and all its suffering officially ended during Commencement Week at the end of May, nearly eleven months after it began. But there would be one final challenge.

A twenty-one-foot granite obelisk, the Herndon Monument, is greased with lard. A Dixie cup sailor hat is glued to the top. The entire plebe class, dressed in regulation p. e. gear, must get the hat, no ladders or equipment allowed. Once the Dixie cup hat is removed, an officer's hat, or "combination cover" is put on top. Then the hazing ends.

It generally takes hours for a class to organize and execute a strategy for climbing Herndon. Hundreds of spectators turn up to watch plebes slip and slide. The Class of 1991, I'm proud to say, climbed Herndon in 43 minutes, 44 seconds, which was a record that still stands today.

To help accomplish this feat, I joined a group of football players and formed with them a base that went all the way around the monument. We allowed smaller classmates to climb on top of us, who in turn let one super tall classmate, Melvyn Davis, climb on top of them. Instead of the normal four-human-length ladder required to reach the top, our class did it with just three.

The ritual completed, plebes were no longer plebes. Just fourth-class midshipmen. Resolved that I would never be hazed again in my life, I walked back to Bancroft Hall with a couple buddies. We had lard smeared over our bodies, and it was time to get cleaned up.

I recall entering the building where, on every weekday afternoon for almost an entire year, I had never actually walked. No plebe was yelling "Go Navy, Sir" or "Beat Army, Sir." No upperclassman was shouting.

The silence was at first bizarre. We, the Class of 1991, would no longer be lined up against the walls. We would never be yelled at again at meals. We felt privileged to ascend the staircase with our hands on the inner railing. We zigzagged down the halls, turning 45 degrees one way and then the other, giggling quietly about it.

There was an airy feeling in my head. In everyone's head. Was it relief?

No.

At that moment of walking peacefully in Bancroft Hall, a moment I will never forget, I felt something I had never felt before in my life.

Humility.

I had been transformed into a new person, stronger and more resilient. But at the same time, more aware of my weaknesses. I had been challenged up to and beyond the point where I met fear of failure and physical pain. I was well acquainted with darkness, loneliness, and inadequacy.

I would never be afraid to suffer myself, and I would never wish ill on another human being again.

After a year and a half, I left the Naval Academy to expand my intellectual horizons and earned a degree in Russian literature at Stanford University. But the lessons learned at the Naval Academy have stayed with me forever.

TAKING RISKS

In the summer between my first and second years as a midshipman, I was assigned training duty on the USS *Cincinnati*, a nuclear attack submarine on a mission in the Mediterranean. I had requested submarine training a few months earlier, after deciding it would be more mysterious and interesting than serving on an aircraft carrier.

Lady Luck was on my side when the faceless assigners put me on the *Cincinnati*. On the week I would embark with her, she would be docked in Sardinia, Italy, getting a bit of repair work done before heading back to Norfolk, her homeport, thirty days later. I would get to visit Europe for the first time. And since the crew was running thin at just around ninety sailors, there would be plenty of opportunity to do real jobs like work in the torpedo room, qualify as a sonar technician, and drive the ship. Another bit of luck for a guy who liked to play with cool toys.

After a week of exercises with the USS *Enterprise* carrier group in the Mediterranean, we parked in Toulouse and, thanks to our skipper who liked midshipmen, I was granted three days of shore leave in France. I gambled in Monte Carlo, looked for topless sunbathers on the beach in Nice, got drunk in a friendly bar, and slept in the train station.

When the boat left Toulouse, we set course for America. We would depart the Mediterranean through the 7.7-mile-wide Strait of Gibraltar.

In another moment of Navy luck, an hour before we passed through the strait, I was recruited by the captain for watch duty in the sail. The sail is the slim wing that sticks up from the middle of a submarine's tubular body. It helps control the submarine as a wing does on an airplane, and it also holds the periscope, snorkel, and radio antennae. There is a small open-air bridge for three or four people, which is accessed by a ladder leading down to the main control room.

It is standard procedure for a watchman to be stationed in the sail when the ship is surfaced and making way. My job that day was to look out for fishing boats and radio down to the control room to avoid collision. The fresh air alone made this job a beauty.

Remarkably ideal weather, 75 degrees, sunny, light seas, and calm winds had inspired the fishermen of Spain and Morocco. And there must have been fish running. Hundreds of small, colorful boats were scattered through the strait that day, each casting nets, trolling, and motoring without fuss.

According to the open water rules of the road, a fishing boat with nets in the water has the right of way over any other kind of ship. So even though we were huge, we had to try to steer clear of these fishing boats. But in real life, small fishing boat drivers understand that a giant submarine is going to ruin their day should a collision occur. My job as watchman, therefore, was pretty simple, as all the boats moved out of our way.

But one boat, a chipped, blue and white twenty-five-footer manned by two olive-skinned, shirtless guys, apparently didn't get the memo. This boat was on a direct course to hit us.

I radioed down, "Sir, there is a fishing boat five hundred yards ahead at ten o'clock."

No response.

I waited a minute or so and tried again, "Sir, there is a boat four hundred yards ahead at eleven o'clock. I think we might hit them."

No response.

There was no one in the sail with me. The protocol was not to leave my post. Nonetheless, I took off my headset and scurried down the ladder. I grabbed the conning officer (in charge of driving the boat) and told him. He checked the periscope and ordered a quick course adjustment. We missed the boat by a couple of hundred feet, a close call by open water standards.

That bit of initiative earned me a pat on the back. The radio man in the bridge had not noticed that his headset had come unplugged. We would have definitely hit that fishing boat if I had not broken protocol and abandoned my post. I took a personal risk because, if the conning officer had been tracking the blue and white boat all along and had another reason not to change course, he would have said to me, "Get back to your post. I know about the goddamn fishing boat."

I wasn't worried about my performance review. It was better to get yelled at than to watch a disaster unfold without trying to prevent it.

This is an important lesson in leadership. **As a leader you have to take action—take risks when necessary, and worry about the repercussions later. You have to be the guy with the courage to do something about the problem.** This lesson would serve me well when I faced a major crisis in the business years later—the story of which is to come.

LONELY AT THE TOP

After the submarine had passed through the Strait of Gibraltar, we set sail for Norfolk, Virginia, the USS *Cincinnati*'s homeport.

It should have been a happy time.

Most crew members had not seen their wives, girlfriends, and children for the better part of a year. Let's just say the men were ready to get reacquainted with the female touch. After being ambassadors in foreign lands, they were looking forward to experiencing the casual comforts of American culture. And, of course, everyone had a food in mind they couldn't wait to eat: real hamburgers, fried chicken, or milkshakes.

Just fifteen easy days' cruise across the pond, and we would all be in paradise.

Only the captain had different plans. Just after we passed through the strait, he let it be known that navy submarine inspectors might be giving the ship a fitness review near Bermuda. This is when admiral types come onto the ship and watch the crew do drills to assess their skill and readiness for battle.

A fitness review at the end of a deployment was unusual. First Class Perry, who taught me how to be a sonar operator, questioned in his Texas drawl, "Why would they give us a fitness review three days before we finish a deployment? That's makes about as much sense as trying to catch a rattlesnake with a ballpoint pen."

A crew being prepared for a fitness review does a lot of drills. Fire drills. Injured sailor drills. Nuclear accident drills.

Whether it made sense or not, every drill started with the siren. Amplified. Then through the ship's loudspeakers, one of which was three feet from my sleeping head, "This is a drill. This is a drill. Emergency. Emergency. There has been a breach in the steam room. Possible nuclear contamination. All hands to emergency stations."

Roused from precious sleep—again—I would slide back my blue cotton privacy curtain, roll out of my rack, put on some clothes, grab an air mask and hose, and head to my emergency station.

We would do at least one major drill every six hours. Nobody on the ship got more than two or three hours of uninterrupted sleep for ten days straight. Tempers on the boat were flaring.

"I swear to God I will strangle the fucking skipper if I see him alone in the engine room."

"Grab your Go Navy butt plugs, boys. It's time for another goddamn drill."

Morale, in the course of a handful of training days, had gone from the heights of the cliffs of Gibraltar to the depths of the Laurentian Abyss.

Once we had sailed past Bermuda, the ten days of training ended. And as most of the crew had predicted, the ship was never inspected. I wondered out loud why the captain had the crew doing all those drills, when it was seemed pretty obvious there was never going to be an inspection.

Chief Robinson, who sat behind me while I manned the helm, gave me his take. "Look, when the crew gets to thinking about home, having sex for the first time in nine months or just fucking off for a few weeks, they start to get sloppy. Yeah, we're not at war, but getting a 360-foot nuclear submarine across the ocean safely requires everyone to stay focused and do their job. If I had to guess, the captain was drilling the shit out of us just to keep us from thinking about how much we are going to enjoy banging our wives when we get back."

I'm sure the captain sat at the small metal desk in his stateroom alone at night and, as he planned the next set of drills, thought to himself, This is a difficult training schedule. The men are not going to enjoy this. They will look me in the eye and say "Aye, aye, sir" but they will want to say "Go fuck yourself, sir."

As a human being, the captain did not enjoy isolating himself from his crew. He simply had no choice. Leading gets in the way of making friends.

I know this from first hand experience. My job at Shopatron is to prepare the company for natural dangers and the brutal attacks of competitors. I want my crew to be the best, for their own good and for mine. The price I pay for success as a leader is loneliness. To correct deficiencies, I make critical comments, harsh judgments, and unpopular decisions.

I keep a running journal in my head of my management team and their strengths and weaknesses. Who follows up and on which matter. Who has golden words but silver deeds. Who is usually wrong and who is usually right.

By now, my vice presidents know that I keep score. And they know that when the time is right, I will reorganize the company to get the right people managing in the right places. Once I have figured out that a vice president cannot execute my vision for a particular part of the company, I relieve him of the responsibility to manage it.

It's understandable my vice presidents choose their words and actions carefully when I am around. My goal is to elevate their performance, not to make them comfortable or be their friend. Stay on your toes. Always do the right thing. You are a vice president, not a janitor.

Being a leader also means being the ultimate decider, whether that is popular or not. It's not unusual for the management team at Shopatron to argue and disagree. I believe conflict, within reasonable bounds, is a natural effect of innovation and rapid growth. Besides structural conflicts (e.g., Sales wants to loosen customer credit terms but Finance wants to tighten credit terms), my vice presidents argue (like professionals would) about priorities, problems, and policies.

When a discussion turns into full on stalemate, and it is clear that consensus cannot be reached, it is my responsibility as CEO to (1) stop the debate so we don't waste time and (2) make a decision. "You both have good points. You both know we have to move forward as a team. You also know it's up to me to make a decision when consensus can't be reached."

George Bush was ridiculed when he said he was "The Decider" in the White House. Of course, he was. I can only imagine how much presidential advisers and policymakers argue inside the White House.

There is a leadership lesson in this: Bush was criticized for stating an obvious fact that he had to decide things as the president. Everyone knows there must be a Decider, but they may not like it—or him. And, this is the important part, the Decider needs to be comfortable with the fact that he may not be liked.

Being a leader also means building a wall between yourself and your employees. I often have access to information, which I cannot share with my staff. Details of weeks-long discussions with lawyers, for example, cannot be explained in full because I just don't have time. Human resource issues demand privacy, which means I can't always say why we terminated an employee. When a competitor reaches out and talks about a partnership or (gasp) a merger, there is no way to share this without creating distraction and disruption.

I must filter and control information in a way that keeps my people focused. In order to be truthful and not misleading, it is often necessary to be terse. One by one, I lay the bricks and create the protective wall that allows me to lead. These bricks do not come down. And as the company gets bigger, the wall gets thicker.

My employees must know the wall is there. They should be able to feel it. I can.

LISTEN OR LEAD

As I'm writing this sentence, it's early morning on Tuesday, November 28, 2011, the day after Cyber Monday.

Robin is still asleep, and it is dark outside.

I am thankful I got a good night's sleep. The holiday season brings loads of online shoppers and with them, massive spikes in page views and orders. I can sleep only if our systems are running smoothly. All of our eighty-four production servers are humming. With sales up a bit more than 40 percent over last year, I am pleased the same way a Formula 1 driver is when his car is fast, blurry fast, and yet trouble free.

High performance is exhilarating, in part because the act of going fast is fun. It's also a rush to know that months or even years of preparation have converged to create a moment when a man-made machine can do so much more than any man could imagine doing alone.

To increase the selection of merchandise we offer, the marketing and sales team signed more than two hundred new merchants in the last year alone. Our online marketing team upgraded more than one hundred existing merchant stores, increasing effectiveness by more than 25 percent. The engineering team optimized our software and servers, ran countless tests to verify system capacity, and stood guard as order volumes grew.

When the season hit, a bigger-than-last-year operations team was ready to wake up early and leave work late, ensuring that every single customer gets a world-class service experience.

All in all, one hundred and thirty-five people acted in concert to make yesterday a record sales day for Shopatron.

A technology company cannot exist without smart, determined people. Change is constant in the technology business. New ideas appear everyday. Our clients depend on us to filter through hundreds of ideas of every month, weeding out the bad ones and, at the same time, adapt very quickly to the good ones.

As new devices (like smart phones and iPads) arrive on the scene, we adapt our software to work on them. When customers change their expectations, we change our solutions.

While this filtering of new ideas is happening, our people also need to operate a business that is growing rapidly. Balancing the operational requirements of a growth company while adapting to rapid change is my main job as the CEO of Shopatron.

It is often unclear in which direction the company should go. And, while I always have an opinion, smart people who work for me have their own ideas. And, as you might expect, many of those ideas are really good. Perhaps better than mine.

Being at the helm, I need to lead the company towards a vision. We need to be synchronized, rowing in the same direction.

But I also need to listen to my people and integrate their new ideas without getting too far off course.

And I need to do this as the technology landscape is continually shifting and morphing, rocking our boat.

Should I listen or should I lead?

Change my vision or "sell" my vision?

Whatever you want to do, Ed.

You asked me for my opinion, Ed.

The hardest aspect of leading a company is knowing, at each decision point, whether it is better to listen to your people or to make them listen to you. I call this the "fence."

Which side of the fence do I want to be on? Should I be on?

I have four simple rules for dealing with the fence.

First, only smart people get to influence my decisions. Once a person has proven him or herself to be careless or sloppy or just plain unintelligent, I ignore their recommendations. Always. The probability of a pay off is too low.

Second, when a smart person is better than me or is an expert at something, I will listen to him almost 100 percent of the time. I get his input on all decisions I make within his subject of expertise. For example, when Sean Collier in our early days insisted that we build Shopatron in a multi-tenant architecture (so all clients would use the exact same software), I deferred to his knowledge of computer systems. When Dave Dalrymple, our VP of engineering until 2010, wanted MySQL as our replacement database for Oracle, the discussion lasted a few minutes. Both of those decisions worked out well for the company, and I didn't spend more than two minutes thinking about them.

Third, if a decision is more tactical than strategic, I encourage my staff to make the decision themselves. If somebody wants to bring me a recommendation or idea for general feedback, I am happy to give it to help him become a better manager of his department. But only if it is not affecting strategy at large and is more an issue of being a helpful manager.

Fourth, if it is not perfectly clear that changing directions will produce better results, I stay the course. Changing direction reduces momentum. It's true with ships, and it's true with businesses.

Knowing when to show clear leadership and make the call and when to be flexible enough to integrate other people's ideas is not an easy skill to master. Being comfortable assessing the quality of ideas is important. But more important is having the humility to accept that another's opinion as better than yours.

Yes, I am pleased Shopatron's servers are running like a top this morning. But, deep inside, I am grateful for the leadership lessons I learned at the Naval Academy, which have allowed me the privilege of leading Shopatron's talented team towards record sales and success.

CHAPTER FOUR
FINANCIAL PARTNERS

While learning the art of leadership in the navy became one of the most important elements of my success at Shopatron, I never had any formal training in the art of finance.

There is no better way to pay the bills than to use actual money earned from customers. Profits. To have a real business, you have to generate profits. But in a start-up company or early stage growth company, profits are elusive and sometimes downright undesirable. If a big, new market is developing and the company is attempting to take a significant share of the market, it might make sense to invest heavily up front. As long as the financial model underlying the business demonstrates that each individual customer is profitable, then the company can operate with losses to gain market share.

This is where investors come in. They provide capital that a business needs, when the business doesn't generate enough cash of its own from customers. For many entrepreneurial ventures, investors are essential to getting a business from the conception of an idea all the way to generating profits years down the road.

As a founder of Shopatron, I traded ownership in my company for capital when it was necessary for the company to take advantage of new market opportunities.

As I mentioned earlier, I raised money to fund Shopatron's growth at four different junctures: 2002, twice in 2004, and in 2007.

I approached fundraising as a young salesman would—with boundless and clumsy enthusiasm and not much in the way of craft.

Despite myself, I got the job done. We always ended up with the money we needed, but much like losing one's virginity, my performance couldn't—in any stretch of the imagination—be described as excellent.

Enthusiastic, yes.

Excellent, no.

As a young entrepreneur, I would be standing at the front of the venture capitalist's conference room. The men with expensive shirts are watching me impatiently. My presentation is flashing on the screen and, occasionally when I step forward to point at something important, my face is illuminated by the projector light.

Questions come fast and furious, interlaced with the subtext of many doubts. It feels like they are throwing spears at me, testing my resolve. My response: never show a weakness.

No, there are not any competitors for this business because we do everything better and newer than anyone.

No, there are no significant risks because this business is protected by me, the warrior who cannot die.

The investors know better, and so they hurl more spears at me. They have seen this story before. Every day they hear another young entrepreneur present on his vision of the future.

The investors sit in their chairs and marvel at me, the entrepreneur, the spectacle.

Does this guy have any idea how unlikely it is that this company will even get off the ground?

How will he possibly compete against the big boys in the market?

Then again, what if he is right about this new market? This could be really big.

After surviving such meetings I learned that investors see the entrepreneur as something that can be possessed. A symbol of investing acumen and status.

A shiny, candy red Ferrari.

Stick with me here. Like a super car, the entrepreneur is attractive to investors.

Investors know a Ferrari will catch the eye of prospective customers and talented employees. He has a lot of horsepower and can move very quickly if needed. He's not built to carry the mail. He's built to carry a billionaire.

But the super car is also dangerous. A Ferrari as CEO is not going to be reliable like a Honda. He's prone to speeding; he is going to be expensive to maintain. Worst of all, a Ferrari is going to cop an attitude and be downright arrogant at times.

And yet a CEO is something an investor cannot make by himself. He must buy a Ferrari in order to have it. How does he do it?

The investor looks at the spreadsheets, the projections, and the market research.

The investor considers carefully his potential return on investment.

The investor looks into every nook and cranny of the business before agreeing to invest.

But all of that is done only after the investor falls in love with the Ferrari. That's right—love.

If there is one thing I have learned in the last ten years and feel compelled to share with all the fundraising virgins out there, it is that feelings and emotions of an investor can never be underestimated. Investors are human beings, first and foremost. They form their basic emotional reaction and decide, in the course of just a few minutes: engage or disengage.

This means you need to have a sexy presentation. Don't be fooled into thinking investors are number scientists who don't care about the way presentations look. They are captivated by colorful graphs and stimulated by repeatedly looking at them.

It is only after they are emotionally engaged, and not long after, that investors become downright analytical.

And after they overcome their initial wonder and awe, this is where all the trouble begins. They begin to soak in all the information and try to figure out what it all means, translating ideas and strategies into dollars and cents: how much money can be made by investing in this business.

As a result, the relationship between entrepreneurs and investors is strained from the start. Entrepreneurs are dreamers, who conceive of something that must be made better in the world. We are optimists. And despite the popularity of the term "serial entrepreneur," most entrepreneurs will have one good idea in their life. We are basically one-shot cannons.

Investors have seen dozens of dreamers like me, and they have lost millions backing them with capital. To investors, dreamers are necessary evils who create new companies, similar to how poopy diapers are part of having children.

But I can tell you that investors do not like dreaming. In fact, they try incredibly hard to invest in companies just exactly at the point in their development when it's clear the dream is going to come true, but before any other investor has figured that out.

COMMUNICATING WITH INVESTORS

After years of stumbling and bumbling, I found the secrets needed to communicate with investors smoothly. I finally came to the understanding that financial controls and reporting are the tools an investor relies upon to understand what is happening with the business. They spend only 1/100th of the time I spend with the business and so they can't be magically confident the business is running well.

And the feelings I get that tell me the business is running well are impossible to translate. In fact, any intuitive confidence I display, without corresponding data to support my confidence, is scary to investors, because they know that entrepreneurs are an optimistic lot.

This happened with our first real financial partner, Rivenrock Capital, run by David Adams and John Nelson, who invested $500,000 in Shopatron in December 2004.

Sean and I did our best to keep our accounting up to snuff, but there were many things we needed to improve. Not least our understanding of net available cash.

There was a period of at least six months where David was trying to explain to us that we were underwater on available cash, and we didn't even know it. He felt we should take additional capital to address the issue, and we did not want to sell more of the company to investors. He got increasingly upset as our balance sheet got weaker and weaker.

He finally protested by refusing to attend board meetings until we addressed the issue. After a profitable holiday season during which we had bolstered our cash position, he came back.

Looking back, I can see how I could have handled that better. David understood our business model at the high level, but it was really only possible to communicate fully with him through the language of finance.

The translation of entrepreneurial confidence from my brain onto a spreadsheet or graph, where it is clear that money will be made: this is the key to communicating with my investors. **Well-presented financial information (with reliable numbers in it) is the best way to truly set a financial investor at ease.**

If I say "We just signed up a big customer," the investor responds, "When will they launch and how much revenue will they produce?" It might have taken all of my heart and soul and months of stressful discussions to sell this big customer, and the first thing I hear from the investor is "Where's my money?"

Throwing an actual bucket of ice-cold water on me would be nicer.

But I've learned that investors don't intend to be negative Nancy. It's just how they are wired, and we have to love them for it.

Another thing we have to love about investors is their obsession with future projections.

Financial investors have two ways to understand the performance of their investment. One, if there is a comparable company in the market (a competitor), then they can compare your performance to its and get a read on how well you are doing. This is pretty difficult in a start-up scenario, because the business is new and unique, so there won't be any comparable companies. Even if there are competitors, they are likely private companies who do not publish their financial data.

Nevertheless, comparisons are always possible with broader sets of companies. Revenue per employee, operating profit, growth rates, etc. Even if "comparable numbers" are not being discussed between the entrepreneur and the investor, rest assured: the company is being compared to other companies by the investors.

The second way investors have to understand the performance of their investment is by looking at actual performance versus the business plan.

In an early stage company, this can be challenging. First, the company doesn't have a refined financial model, so making accurate projections is hard. Sean and I would take our best guess at sales and revenue and project that. When something went wrong, or if revenue was more volatile than we expected, we figured the investors would understand.

That is funny now. Because financial investors never understand missed projections.

Financial investors get upset when projections are not hit, even if the business overall is still doing very well, as they worry that the business is underperforming.

As the company gets bigger, you need to be able to hit projections. It makes the company more valuable if you can demonstrate that you understand it well enough to project accurately. No one wants to buy into a volatile business. It's a comfort thing.

People told me, just estimate lower. Sandbag your plan. That is well and good, except we were creating the future with this company. I wanted my staff to think big and push for the most. It's hard to get a start-up group of ten people to be thinking about changing the world ("this is going to be huge!") and then sandbag the results. (Well, yes, we are going to change the world, but let's plan to change the world 50 percent less just to be conservative.)

So I never sandbagged for the first nine years or so when creating projections at Shopatron. What can I say? I was young and dumb.

I remember during 2009–2010, in the pit of recession, we were growing at 45 percent annually, but the investors were concerned because I had projected the growth to be higher. They expressed their concern in a Board meeting once—let's just say in an unambiguous yet respectful way. I thought, wow, these guys really value accurate forecasting. And that's when it hit me that we needed to forecast more conservatively.

As our business has grown, it has actually become easier to project and hit forecasts. It is still impossible to forecast big, new product launches, but I try my best to speak the investors' language. And by speaking their financial language, I have picked up more than a few tips on how to run the company better.

I am pretty sure my investors appreciate it when I communicate with them in financial terms, the same way that the French waiter smiles a bit when you try to order your dinner in broken French. A little bit of cultural respect goes a long way.

GRANDPA'S MISTAKE

During the times when my relationships with investors were most strained, I would wonder if getting investors was the right thing to do in the first place.

Not only did I not have any formal training on how to work with financial partners, I did not have any role models to help me understand how to work with them. In fact, all of my uncles and my dad, my only real business role models, had always been focused on controlling 100 percent of their businesses.

My family—both sides—was comprised of first and second generation immigrants. Our last name, Stevens, was changed from Stefanik at Ellis Island when my great-grandparents immigrated from Poland to America. Stevens sounded like an English name; all the better to avoid discrimination.

My grandparents had no support network in America (like most immigrants). Not yet integrated culturally as "Americans," they relied on their wits and work ethic. Self-sufficiency was their key success strategy.

My great-grandfather was a furniture deliveryman in New York before the days when trucks were used. He was a giant man who pushed a cart full of furniture from the store to customers' homes and who could carry any piece of furniture single-handedly up as many flights of stairs as needed, as the legend goes.

My grandfather, Frank Stevens, considered himself an American success story. He grew up poor and uneducated, never graduating from eighth grade. As a young man, Frank took up boxing and fought his way around the Midwest as a semi-pro.

I don't have any reason to doubt that he was a capable fighter. Even when he was eighty years old, he had large muscled forearms and a glint in his eye that begged for conflict.

As he got on in years, Frank Stevens still loved talking about how he built his business. When I was a young boy visiting his house on a Sunday afternoon, it made me happy to see him reminisce about his life's journey.

By one of his accounts, he was looking for a job desperately in the Depression. He had settled in Cleveland to chase the woman who would become my grandmother. A position as a truck driver for a furniture store was advertised in the newspaper. He showed up to apply, and there were hundreds of men crowded around the door. My grandfather shoved his way to the front and, just as he got to the door, the man inside said no more applicants would be accepted. My grandfather stuck his forearm into the door and, despite the man repeatedly closing the door on it, he kept his arm in the door. Admiring Frank's persistence as much as his pain threshold, the man let him in.

Frank told the interviewer that he knew how to drive a truck (which was not true). When he got to the warehouse to start his first day's work, he convinced the other drivers to teach him how to drive a truck. It was no problem. That's how Frank operated.

At some later point in his furniture career, my grandfather had taken a job as a stock boy at a small furniture store. One day, the owner left to run an errand and told him to watch the store. As luck would have it, a newlywed couple came in, looking for a house full of furniture. Frank showed the couple around the store and would not let them leave, despite their multiple attempts to walk out. To kill time, he pretended to show them features and benefits of the furniture, talked to them about their home, and so on. More than an hour later, the owner returned.

It didn't take long for the owner to make the sale. As the paperwork was being finished, the couple asked if the young man would be getting a commission. The puzzled owner of the store asked, "Why should a stock boy get a commission?" They told the owner that Frank was helpful in selecting the furniture, and further that he would not let them leave the store.

The owner told Frank to go home and put on a tie. He became a furniture salesman that day.

Eventually Frank opened his own store, Factory Furniture. By the middle of the 1960s, Factory Furniture was the largest chain of furniture stores in Cleveland. My grandfather had gone from truck driver to being the number one furniture man in town. Not bad for a guy who never graduated from eighth grade.

My grandfather was a scrappy guy who made it from nobody to somebody, but his one mistake was that he was obsessed with controlling his business. What made him successful in the first place, his self-sufficiency, worked against him as his business grew. He did not have the capacity to trust and was unable to scale his furniture business.

He did have five stores at one point. With four sons, Frank's vision was for each to manage a satellite store while he managed the main store. He convinced some of his sons to skip college, so they could focus their career working for him. My dad ended up going to college and law school, but he had to resist his own father's exhortations to pull that off.

When Frank's sons got tired of working in the satellite stores, they opened their own stores. Frank lost his managers and couldn't really replace them because he had not developed any management systems. Only family could be trusted to manage a store, not a "stranger who would steal."

As he got older and his sons left his empire, the satellite stores closed one by one, ending up with one final store in downtown Cleveland, just a shadow of his former empire. When Frank died, his business died with him.

The ending of the story makes me sad, thinking about those stores shutting down, boarded-up windows, showrooms empty of furniture. Yet Frank's life and work also has given me a deep insight that has helped me grow Shopatron.

While it often does take singular vision and drive to get a new business off the ground, the entrepreneur must adapt and wean himself of the magic ego elixir known as control—if he wants to grow his business to any considerable size. Building a big business requires skill and experience beyond the capacity of any one mortal. Ambitious, talented people, who are the rocket fuel for any company's growth, will not stay at a business where the owner is an untrusting micromanaging control freak.

As I have evolved from an entrepreneur to a CEO of a growth company, I have had to give up control in two ways. First, as I discussed in the previous chapter, I give my dedicated, smart, and capable managers the room to lead their groups and be in command of their part of the business, including accepting the mistakes they make. Sometimes giving power and control to subordinates is called "delegating." It's not my favorite word, since it conjures the notion that I am giving my staff small and unimportant things to do, which I don't want to do myself. I delegate control and with it, responsibility.

The other form of control I have had to give up is with my ownership of the company.

When I started Shopatron, I owned 88 percent of it. I had the controlling percentage of shares in the company. Any decision I wanted to make, I could make. None of my minority partners could have stopped me.

After creating a stock option pool for some of our early employees, and after our various funding rounds in 2002 and 2004, my ownership dropped to 54 percent. Still, I had majority control of the company's shares.

By early 2007, however, the time had come for the business to raise additional capital to accelerate its growth and expand into Europe. I needed to bring on another financial partner who would invest three to six million dollars. In exchange for his money, the new investor would want 20 percent to 40 percent of the company. My ownership stake would fall below 51 percent, and I would no longer be "in control."

THE PERFECT FIT

For anyone who is new to financing, a company's stock can be organized into any number of classes, each with its own set of voting rules and rights. Common stock is generally structured as the vanilla class of stock. Plain and simple ownership of the company with no special rights. All of the family and friends investors, the co-founders like Sean Collier, and I own Shopatron common stock.

When we raised our money in 2004 from Rivenrock, we created a "Series A" preferred class of stock. Rivenrock got about 10 percent of the company with its stock purchase, which normally would not confer any special control (other than having one-tenth of the voting power). By creating the Series A class with a few special rights, though, we gave them a permanent seat on the Board of Directors and a few key rights related to future company financings. Series A shareholders also were given a guaranteed 2x liquidation preference, with seniority. As Series A shareholders, they were guaranteed to double their money before common stock shareholders made a penny.

These rights attached to our Series A stock were, more or less, conventional. Most professional investors do deals that have similar terms. I never had a problem with the terms as I still controlled the fate of the business, and Shopatron could not raise money, make investments, or change strategic directions without my support. I believed in the business, and so I was confident the protective provisions would never need to be used.

When I went out to raise our big round of capital in 2007, I would be selling Shopatron's soon-to-be-created Series B stock. Together with Sean, I put together a business plan, which included our historical financial information, future projections, and market landscape analysis. We were seeking $3 to $6 million, and we stated three primary uses for the money:

1. Expand our sales and marketing operation in the United States,
2. Open a European office, and
3. Increase investment in new products, especially in-store pickup of online orders, which I viewed then (and still do) as the biggest opportunity in eCommerce.

I sent our business plan to ten prospective investors for review. In each case, there was at least cursory interest in Shopatron. Phone calls were held. Presentations were given. Data were analyzed.

Four of the ten prospective investors got serious, which means that they sent me a summary term sheet, outlining the basic aspects of an investment offer.

One investor was a Boston-based venture capital firm. The lead partner who started discussions with me was brilliant, humble, and experienced. His term sheet wasn't the best of the four, but his profile as an investor and board member was. Unfortunately, once the term sheet was delivered, he relegated the deal to a junior guy on his staff. I may have done the deal if the lead partner was going to lead the investment and be a real mentor over the course of our relationship with his firm. I didn't think a freshly-minted MBA would have enough experience to be my mentor, though, so I looked elsewhere for a partner.

Another term sheet came from a really impressive Boston-based individual who had been the CEO of a brand that used Shopatron. He offered the highest valuation on Shopatron as a company, and he was an incredibly capable businessman. His downfall was that he really wanted to be the CEO of Shopatron, or at least control the company extensively. For some time, I considered his implication that I wasn't the right CEO for Shopatron. Then, I decided to pass on his offer.

The third term sheet was from a Santa Barbara-based venture capital firm. It was partnered up with a number of bright and well-connected technology entrepreneurs in Southern California. And, it seemed to have the most support from my Series A investor, David from Rivenrock. Unfortunately, its valuation of Shopatron was by far the lowest.

The last term sheet we reviewed came from a newly formed private equity firm based in San Francisco, called Kern Whelan. J. P. Whelan, a co-founder of the firm, was a teammate of mine on the Stanford rugby team. He and his partner, Jay Kern, practiced a method of investing which appealed to me as an entrepreneur.

Unlike the other firms, Kern Whelan was adamant that the legal terms and interests of all holders of stock—Common, Series A, or Series B—should be aligned. Kern Whelan believed it was important for all the shareholders to work as a team and that mutual trust was critical to long-term success. Thus, no special protective provisions were in its offer. Management could spend and borrow without explicit approval, and we could make business decisions freely.

Kern Whelan's source of funding, syndication, was attractive, too. This means it syndicated each investment deal to a network of high net worth individuals, who decided for themselves to invest or not invest. This is different than in a venture capital fund, which has money pre-raised from limited partners sitting in the bank and ready for instant deployment.

It might seem like a minor difference, but the implications are huge.

For one, venture capital firms typically have five to ten partners, who all must approve an investment. While their capital is pre-raised (an advantage), the process for releasing it to companies involves a fair amount of internal politics. If one partner doesn't like the investment, or has a conflicting investment, the venture capital firm won't invest or will offer crappy terms.

In a syndicated deal done by a small firm like Kern Whelan, there are perhaps two partners who approve the deal, and then it is released to the high net worth individuals for funding. If one of the high net worth individuals doesn't like the deal, he can't veto it. He just doesn't invest, and the deal moves forward with other investors.

The other reason I like syndicated deals is that there is no clock ticking.

Venture capitalists raise their funds in ten-year chunks. A couple of hundred million dollars, for example, is invested into the venture capital fund by pension funds, university endowment funds, the super rich, and the like. A limited partnership is formed, outlining how the money will be invested and when it will be returned. In most cases, the partnership is given a ten-year life. When ten years is reached, all investments the venture capital fund has made must be wrapped up, so all the capital can be returned to the limited partners, together with their share of the profits.

Ten years seems like a long time, but it really isn't.

When a venture capital fund closes its fund, the clock starts ticking. They have ten years to find a couple of dozen great companies to invest in, help those companies mature into valuable growth companies, then sell the companies. In reality, they make their investments in years one through three of the fund. They weed out the losers and make follow-on investments in the winners in years four through seven. They are working to sell or exit the investments in years eight through ten.

The reputation venture capitalists have for always wanting to "exit" or "liquidate" their companies has nothing to do with their personality types. It has everything to do with the structure of their funding. Unless you are lucky enough to get investment from a fund in its year one, you are looking at about five years' maximum runway before the venture capitalists become obsessed with selling you.

To bring this all back to Shopatron, I chose Kern Whelan out of the bunch, partly because it was organized to syndicate our deal, rather than invest in it from a clock-ticking fund. I also chose it because it understood our future vision.

Five years is not a lot of time to change the world. I wanted Shopatron to change the world, but I wasn't sure it could do it in five years.

By 2007, we had a network of more than five thousand retailers across America fulfilling online orders for manufacturers—one of the larger distributed fulfillment networks in the world. We built the network to solve channel conflict for manufacturers, but it could be leveraged to do much more.

I could see it coming, like a freight train, that consumers in the future would want to order online and pick up their online order in a store. Circuit City, a now defunct consumer electronics retailer, was already offering in-store pickup. The data were staggering: more than 30 percent of Circuit City's online shoppers picked up their online orders in a Circuit City store.

It made sense that national retailers would be the first to offer in-store pickup. They had their own network of stores, with unified computer systems that could handle the management of the orders from online checkout through the local pickup.

Yet many manufacturers could not build this kind of capability themselves. They would need to buy software to do it. Shopatron had the opportunity to transform our technology to service this new group of customers. Manufacturers would use Shopatron not just because they didn't want to compete with their retailers. They would use Shopatron because consumers wanted to pick up online orders locally. And since manufacturers couldn't possibly have a store in every city, it meant they would need to integrate with retailers as order fulfillment partners.

Shopatron had to grow faster, to increase our footprint of fulfillment locations. We had to build robust in-store pickup technologies. The capital raise of 2007 was for both of those purposes.

The tricky thing was that the optimal timing of the opportunity was not clear. How long would it take for consumers to expect to be able to have in-store pickup at a manufacturer website? Wouldn't Amazon deliver products so quickly to consumers that local pickup would be irrelevant?

How would retailers be integrated into this big network? Would inventory be required from every retailer? How is that even possible?

To align the realities of the market with our finance strategy, I needed an investor who:

A. liked our core "channel conflict" business and believed it would grow at least into a nice $100 million business,

B. understood that in-store pickup (web to store) was a giant, billion-dollar opportunity,

C. had the ability to be somewhat patient while the in-store pickup opportunity developed in the market and while we developed the solutions to make it actually work (i.e., did not have a fund with the clock ticking),

D. was incredibly smart, very experienced, and fully engaged with my business and, most importantly,

E. was somebody whom I trusted enough to take my ownership below 51 percent.

Kern Whelan hit all these points, and I chose it, even though its valuation was second best of the four offers. I am so glad now that I was not looking just for money. I was looking for the right partner and selected it. That goes down as one of my best decisions ever.

STAYING IN CONTROL

Getting the deal done required an astonishing amount of time and energy, most of it spent after I selected Kern Whelan.

I had to talk and talk and talk and discuss and discuss and discuss and then push and push and push to get the deal done. It was a full time job. Ten hours a day, reading documents, making phone calls, and working out solutions to roadblocks.

But it was worth it and by August 2007, the Series B deal closed. With Riven-rock and several existing investors choosing to join the round and buy deeper into Shopatron, we ended up at the high end of our expected range on the financing. We had raised $5.9 million.

It looked pretty darn good on the bank statement. $5,900,000.

Knowing we had been funded for our full business plan, plus over a million dollars in reserves, Sean and I did what any entrepreneurs would do.

Hire.

A lot.

Of People.

We had about thirty employees at Shopatron when we closed the Series B deal. By March 2008, we had fifty-five. We brought in ten new salespeople, a manager for them, a couple new vice presidents and directors to manage finance and client services, and five more software engineers. We even hired a full-time recruiter to help us fill open positions.

Although we loved our fifty-five-hundred-square-foot space near downtown San Luis Obispo, it could not be expanded to house the one hundred employees we expected to have by the end of 2008. We negotiated a buyout of our lease and rented a new space across town, which was a little more than seventeen thousand square feet. To get our European market entry started, we got an office in England and put a half dozen people there.

It wasn't just payroll and rent that went up. Expenses for computers, software, and office supplies increased in line with our employee count.

We spent more on travel as well. Staff members were flying to England and back for training. More salespeople traveling. More phones. More everything.

An expansion driven by an insertion of equity is meant to increase costs. That's why the money is needed in the first place. More people and investment in growth leads to higher revenues down the road. Yet while that investment is getting started, the company will run operating losses. On paper the company looks worse, but in reality it is getting a whole lot better.

By bringing in Kern Whelan and its capital, we had strengthened the company and given it a higher chance of overall success. But I had weakened the amount of power I personally had over the company.

We had increased the number of seats on our board of directors to five. Now my shares were good enough to vote myself on the board, but not good enough for controlling a majority of three seats. Technically, three directors could vote to fire me as CEO at any time.

This is the position into which my grandfather, my father, and all the male role models I had growing up would have never let themselves get. Frank surely would have been disappointed in me.

I could almost hear him saying, "Eddie, never ever give anybody any control of your business. You have to control it yourself to do it right."

The truth is, though, you don't have to control 100 percent of the shares of a company to be in control of the company. The pilot of a 747 is in control of the plane; he doesn't become the captain through ownership. He earns the privilege to command through training and diligence. He is in charge of the plane only if he remains competent.

As the pilot of Shopatron, there are many vectors I must manage at once: intellectual and emotional, internal and external, short term and long term. Too many to list.

I have to keep everyone working together. Investors, managers, employees. We all want the same thing.

Grow the business.

Expand the branded manufacturer solution into more industries and more countries. Make it a scalable growth business anyone would be proud to own. Be true to the thousands of customers who use that solution everyday to drive their revenue. Shopatron is important to them. Live up to their expectations and more.

There are a handful of tricks I've picked up over the years that help me maintain my command of the company.

First, I never drink my own Kool-Aid alone. People have to drink it with me. Any crazy new idea must be validated. My scheduled weekly call with investors gives me a safe format for bouncing ideas back and forth. Big decisions, like those that have price tags over six figures, are always good to validate with managers and Board members. Ultimately, I need to make most decisions, but my stakeholders like knowing why I am doing things. Often, they help me refine a decision to deliver a better outcome for the company.

Equally, though, I never ask a Board member what he wants me to do. I come to the table with a recommendation, then get feedback. I change my decision only if the feedback is compelling.

Harking back to my Naval Academy days, if I don't know the answer to something, I always say "No excuse" and "I'll find out." I take responsibility for the things that go wrong. The buck stops with me. It has to.

At Board meetings, I must not be defensive. Board members are there to help me. They implicitly support me (since I have my job); I must not feel insecure about feedback and criticism. It works well to say, "Thanks. I had not thought of that." And write down the note for future contemplation.

I let the management team know that my job is every bit as performance based as theirs. If I perform poorly, I am out. This strengthens me at moments when I make unpopular decisions. My managers know that one bad decision could cost me my job. Clearly, I haven't made a big mistake yet. I have my job because I deserve it.

I abhor nepotism and weird favoritisms. I treat myself the way an executive should expect to be treated, no better or worse. I fly coach because they fly coach. Overall it makes the business stronger and more robust—more corporate in that the company is not Ed. The company is Shopatron and it will continue on with or without Ed.

I assume my strongest supporters on the Board will turn on me in an instant should my performance fail to meet their expectations. They might really like me. But they will remove me as CEO without shedding a tear if they think it is in the best interests of the company they invested in.

All of these things keep me in line and focused on striving to be the best performing CEO possible. When the Series B deal was inked, however, I hadn't figured all of these things out. And, much to my dismay, my performance as CEO was tested much sooner than I would have liked.

As we were closing the Series B deal, the first signs of economic collapse showed up. That's right. The markets for CDO's (Collateralized Debt Obligations), the mortgage financing instruments that caused the run up in housing prices, started falling apart in August 2007. Just as we were closing our deal.

During the deal and in the months afterwards, I didn't think too much about this. I had just completed a nine-month process and was focused on making Shopatron one of the most important eCommerce companies in the world.

I had no idea that the Great Recession was on the horizon.

The Trans Am that I got when I was sixteen—and totaled six days later. The day after the wreck, my dad made me go to work at the family furniture store where he told me that by selling one additional sofa, I'd pay for the bump in insurance premium.

My years at the US Naval Academy were brutal, but it was there that I learned what makes a truly great leader: humility.

My post-collegiate years in Russia included many nights in the *banya*, or sauna, drinking vodka and bonding with the guys. Living in Russia makes it clear that material wealth is not necessary for happiness.

My college girlfriend, Robin—now my wife of twenty years and the mother of my two children—was crazy enough to move to Russia with me after she graduated from Stanford, and she has been by my side ever since. People ask me how I have been able to deal with all of the financial risks that accompany entrepreneurship. It's simple. I know my wife will love me no matter what, so I have nothing to lose—just money.

My grandfather, Frank Stevens. He was a successful entrepreneur and yet also had shortcomings that I've tried to avoid.

As a midshipman in Annapolis, Maryland, with my oldest and youngest brothers, Cliff and Joe—a day away from the chaos and challenges of the US Naval Academy.

My desk at the military factory in St. Petersburg, where I worked after graduating from college with a degree in Russian literature. No Herman Miller chair, and a rotary phone to boot. I used an acoustic coupler to connect to the United States by modem.

Happy New Year at work in Russia. It was 1993 and the year of the rooster. It took a lot of scrubbing in the bathtub to make my shirt that white!

Picking stones and bugs out of the rice Robin and I bought at a street market in St. Petersburg in 1993. Life in Russia was tough but never boring.

Some of my colleagues and I enjoying a midday work celebration complete with cognac, champagne, and salami. Drinking at work was rare, actually, and the team was hard-working.

One of my hobbies while living in Russia was buying and collecting paintings and drawings. My comrade Vasily Petrovich (middle) and I are working down prices while the seller explains how artists need to have money to eat. All negotiating tactics are fair in Russia.

My family and I at the Santa Barbara Triathlon. One of the core values at Shopatron is "family first."

Some members of the Shopatron team at the City to the Sea half marathon in San Luis Obispo. At Shopatron, we promote healthy activities, teamwork, and leadership through various sporting events.

CHAPTER FIVE
WRAPPING PAPER

My great-grandmother, Katherine Griesebach, was most famous in my family for her frugality. She rode a giant tricycle to the grocery store, throughout her seventies and eighties because cars were too expensive and exercise was healthy anyway. She lived in a modest house in a suburb of Cleveland, and she drank a glass of wine every night—purchased by the case, of course, because of the discount.

When we would get together at my grandmother's house for Christmas, which we did every year, Katherine would turn up and watch the festivities from an oversized white wing chair, the most comfortable seat in the house. We opened presents from youngest to oldest, so Katherine always opened her presents last.

Twenty or so grandchildren would sit around Katherine's chair, ready for the annual spectacle. She would take a present, rotate it slowly and examine how it was wrapped. When she had completed her survey of the wrapping job, she would carefully insert fingers—or scissors if needed—into one of the folds, being sure not to tear it.

Then she would disassemble the entire wrap job, holding the paper up in front of her, proud like a farmer holding up a giant zucchini for show. She then proceeded to fold the paper neatly. That's right. She folded the wrapping paper so she could save it and use it again.

We thought it was weird to save wrapping paper. We thought she was taking the whole save-your-pennies thing a bit too far.

I'm not so sure anymore.

Katherine had seen her fair share of tough times. She was thirty-three years old when the Great Depression started in 1929.

A lot has been said about the generation that lived through the Great Depression. "Clean your plate" doesn't make sense as a parenting technique in 2012, when half of Americans are obese. But if you have ever been hungry for weeks on end, you will clean your plate and tell your children to do the same for the rest of your life.

You might start saving the wrapping paper off presents, too.

THE GREAT RECESSION

While most of us have not lived through the extreme hardships of the Great Depression, many of us did experience the Great Recession of 2008–2009—a time of enormous struggle, caused by a steep and shocking contraction of economic activity around the world. By a wide margin, the Great Recession was the biggest economic contraction since the Great Depression.

A collapse of the housing market got the whole thing started. Home prices, which had run up to historic highs and beyond, began to fall in 2006. Financial instruments that underpinned mortgage markets fell in concert. Giant banks and financial services companies, which had bet on the housing market's continued rise, lost huge amounts of money. Their insolvency tossed the entire financial system into danger.

Stock markets were hit hard as investors fled for safety. In the fall of 2008, markets careened down. The Dow Jones Industrial Average fell more than 40 percent in September and October.

Americans watched their primary assets, homes and stocks, plummet in value. Anvils were falling from the sky, and nobody knew where to hide. Fear took over. People stopped spending. Then companies stopped spending.

From the fourth quarter of 2007 to the second quarter of 2009, the US Gross Domestic Product (GDP), the economy's overall size, shrunk by 4.1 percent, and millions of Americans lost their jobs. The unemployment rate doubled to 10.1 percent.

I watched the news and read the blogs throughout the whole ordeal. Every day there seemed to be a surprise, a new worry, another asset class losing value.

Banks tightened lending. Government debt increased. Political gridlock prevented growth-oriented reforms. Consumers pulled back spending. Business conditions got much tougher for branded manufacturers and retailers, which of course, affected Shopatron.

At the very beginning of the Great Recession in 2008, I didn't even know it had begun. There was media coverage on the fall in housing prices, but plenty of pundits were arguing the economy would continue to grow. A federal stimulus in the form of tax rebate in the second quarter was supposed to provide an adequate boost to the economy.

My bias (I am an entrepreneur, after all) was with the optimists. I had just raised $5.9 million from new investors. I was expected to deliver strong revenue growth regardless of economic conditions. Maybe there would be some obstacles ahead. I accepted it as part of the grow-a-big-company adventure I signed up for.

Experiencing the Great Recession as Shopatron's CEO was an adventure, that's for sure. Not a swashbuckling hero adventure, though, more like a creepy science fiction movie. I was the lead character, the captain of a shiny new spaceship, commanding his first extraterrestrial mission.

In this Shopatron-meets-Recession sci-fi flick, true to its genre, everything starts out just fine. The crew is excited to be embarking on the journey. Space is full of wonderful and beautiful planets and quasars. Jokes are told, and cool new technologies are on display.

This is what Shopatron felt like in August 2007, right after we raised our Series B financing. Our mission to conquer the eCommerce universe had begun. We had plenty of money, energy, and purpose. All systems were go.

Then the commander begins to notice a few anomalies. A strange event is followed by another. One of the crew members is behaving oddly. The ship seems to be slowing down, even though the engines are on full power. Nobody knows why.

Even an inexperienced CEO can tell the business is not tracking the way it should. The business plan and financial model, the operating manuals for your business, contain no helpful diagnoses. Your top lieutenants have no answers. The higher-ups in the boardroom fail to mention that their other portfolio companies are encountering unexplained resistance, too.

In our case, it was our transaction revenue, the piece of every sale that we make when an order passes through our order exchange, that kept missing targets. No matter what we did to increase transaction revenue, our efforts failed to make an impact.

The ramp-up of our sales team, which was one of the primary uses of the $5.9 million we raised, was taking too long. It took longer to hire new salespeople, and they took longer to become productive. Maybe we made some bad hires, we thought. Maybe the customers we were acquiring were too small.

Merchants who had promised to launch Shopatron in Europe delayed or postponed their schedule. Those that did launch produced a lot less transaction revenue than we had hoped.

We did not have any plausible explanations for our slowdown. The business had not developed a set of comprehensive metrics to understand itself yet. (More on that later.)

The six-month period from January to June 2008 felt like a time warp.

And take it from me: time does not fly when you are not having fun.

Finally, by the third quarter of 2008, however, it became clear that our transaction revenue was falling short because of a dramatic drop in consumer spending. The housing crisis was going to take a big bite out of the US economy, after all.

It was reassuring in a way to understand the enemy. A recession. I had seen a few of those before.

And if the recession had been normal in any way, we could have dealt with it without too much pain and suffering.

But this recession was like the nasty alien that is way smarter, faster, more powerful, and uglier than any you have faced before. In the middle of 2008, when the recession still felt "normal" to us at Shopatron, we were taking actions like deciding not to re-wallpaper our office and slowing down a few peripheral hires. We had raised an extra $1 million for contingencies just like this, and we continued to execute our expansion plan without disruption.

No little recession is going to take this commander off his game.

Well that didn't last long.

When the presidential election kicked into full gear in the fall, all hell broke loose. In September and October, the stock market plummeted. GM and Chrysler went broke. And a few giant banks were hastily rolled into other giant banks, which were supposed to be solvent.

The thing I remember most from this time was fear.

For starters, my investors were afraid.

Not about Shopatron specifically, as whatever suspicions they might have had concerning Shopatron's lack of performance in early 2008, or my performance for that matter, disappeared in the fog of battle.

It was just not a good time for them generally with the stock market crash, the housing crash, and the banking crash. Fortunes were being lost and companies were dying. In our Board meetings, we talked about cash protection and circling wagons.

They weren't the only ones. Customers were also afraid.

By late 2008 and early 2009, most of our clients were reporting sales drops on the order of 20 to 30 percent. Online sales with Shopatron were flat, but the rest of their businesses were in a free fall.

In the spring of 2009, we canceled our client conference. Few of our clients had the money to attend. We didn't want to spend the money on it, either.

Seeing and hearing of the carnage our customers were experiencing, our employees got afraid, too. They didn't have to tell me they were afraid. I could see it in their eyes. The majority of Shopatron's costs were (and still are) in people, which is typical in the software business. Our employees were afraid for their jobs and for their families.

But Shopatron was never in danger of going out of business. In fact, we were growing at a 45 percent clip during the Great Recession. Our revenue was growing fast, but running below target. As a result of the investment we had made in expansion, we were running losses. Thus in order to start showing a profit again, we needed to consider the level of investment in further growth and how that played into our overall cash balance. How much should we invest in sales and marketing? How many engineers do we want working on new products? Should we continue to build our presence in Europe?

Raising new capital was an option, but a poor one in the middle of a global economic meltdown. Better to make sure the company would get back to profitability sooner rather than later.

After exhaustive analysis and consultation with Board members, I had to make just one decision to navigate the Great Recession. To get the company back to break even, I had to choose to scale back investment in one of these three areas: European expansion, new product development, or sales and marketing.

Europe was in some ways the easy pick. It was costing us $100,000 a month with almost no revenue in return. In every Board meeting and phone call, there would be hard questions about Europe. Here's a real example: "So, Ed, maybe it's something with me, something I don't understand, but can you please tell me why the fuck we are still investing all this money in Europe?"

We didn't open an office in Europe to make a quick buck, though. We opened an office there because our customers said it was important to them. They wanted a global platform to lower operating costs across multiple divisions, brands, and distributors.

More importantly, I knew that the order exchange was Shopatron's best asset. It took eight years to build it in the United States, and it would take time in Europe, but would harvest many returns. I was not going to lose that big opportunity.

Scaling back investment in new product development was a tempting option, too.

When spending on new product development is reduced, the company still continues to make the same revenue in the short term. Therefore, it is the easiest path to profitability. But it's also the deadliest path for a software company. Technology never stops moving, and customers expect their software to be up to date, especially anything that faces the end consumer.

Cut new product development now. Die a slow death later.

In the end, I decided to pull back our sales and marketing investment by 50 percent. Shopatron's growth rate would slow down for a couple years as a result, but we would get back to break even while continuing to invest in future technologies and in Europe.

A contributing factor to the decision was that our sales and marketing operation was not as efficient as we wanted. After we reduced head count and spending, we would have a cleaner slate on which to redesign the departments for larger scale.

Probably the most difficult period of my professional life was the third quarter of 2009, when we restructured our sales and marketing group. It was painful to undo the investment we had made just one year earlier. Some really good people were asked to leave the company.

One day, I was talking to a senior sales executive about his prospective new customers. The next day, I was telling him, by phone no less, that his services were no longer required by the company. Hearts and souls were broken. Mine included. Some people were hurt more than others, and some may not have even deserved their fate.

When someone says to you, "Ed, I can't believe you're doing this to me," there is no response that makes it feel better.

Only thinking that it is for the good of the company. For the rest of us whose families rely on the company to be healthy.

For Shopatron and me, the restructuring of the sales and marketing team was the last major battle of the Great Recession. Like all battles, it was messy and didn't go exactly as I had planned. Letting go of half the sales and marketing team was a blunt trauma to Shopatron. It could have knocked us down, but it didn't. The remaining team rallied together and played the roles we asked of them. The company had to move forward with a viable cost structure, and that was that.

For a couple weeks after the restructuring, I felt just plain tired and down in the dumps. I had done what needed to be done, and yet there was so much work ahead.

Then I thought about how my mom and dad motored through tough times at the Furniture Depot. To reenergize myself, I drew once more from the lessons of my youth.

I had heard resiliency in Dad's voice when I would ask, "How was business today? Did you sell a lot of furniture?" "No, we had just one small sale today. A nightstand. It's rough out there, Eddie. But we'll get it back tomorrow."

When times got really tough, we would cut back at home, do more with less, and apply a little more elbow grease. Eat out less. Skip that vacation we had been hoping to take.

I told myself, just buckle down and make as much progress as you can. When tomorrow comes, you're going to be glad you didn't give up today.

SEA CHANGES

Turn back the clock to the summer of 1988. I am in the middle of the Caribbean Sea on a sailboat called *America's Promise*. We are Naval Academy midshipmen on a summer training cruise, heading to St. Lucia, one of the southern-most islands in the West Indies.

Although it is only one day into our cruise, it looks like we are going to get baptism by fire. The clouds are gathering on the horizon, and the radio says a tropical storm lies ahead. The sun is setting over our right shoulders as we point south.

We rush below and put on rain suits as the wind picks up.

The captain orders the jib to be lowered and our main sail to be reefed. Less sail area exposed to the wind reduces the chance that a strong gust will capsize our sixty-foot sloop.

The temperature drops as the front moves towards us. Raindrops fall on our fresh, crinkly gear. The boat, which had seemed so big just one day earlier, heaves high and low as she crashes through the sea.

Salt water hits my lips when the spray across the bow flies into the cockpit. Adrenaline surges through my body as the officers shout commands.

This is no drill.

We are in the middle of the ocean, and no other human beings are within sight. If we make a mistake, it might be our last.

It feels like I am on a roller coaster ride without an end. Up and down. Pitch and splash. More salt water on my face.

An hour into the storm, I've been given the helm. It's hard to hold a course, but I try my best. I'm the only midshipman who hasn't thrown up. The rest are green faced and hanging over the leeward rail, puking their dinner into the dark.

Suddenly I realize that, while I was afraid earlier, I am no longer so.

I have figured out that our sloop is not in seas beyond her design. She is handling everything this storm is giving her.

In every storm, there is that moment when you realize that you are going to make it through. In a sailboat, it's when the waves and wind have peaked and you can tell the boat is stable and the rudder still works.

After a few more hours, the waves give up their relentless growth, and the wind, too. We sail onward to our destination, a slightly more seasoned crew than twelve hours earlier.

I felt this same way managing Shopatron through the Great Recession, the moment just after our sales and marketing teams had been restructured. We were lean enough and mean enough, ready for anything the economic storm still had in store for us. The company was positioned to operate profitably and to grow at a still-pretty-healthy growth rate. We had our hand on the tiller, ready to continue our adventure.

The weather ahead was looking fairer. It was clear by early 2009 that the world as we knew it was not going to melt into oblivion. The governments had stepped in and bailed out the banks, the car companies, anyone who needed it. There was plenty of doom and gloom in the media, but disaster had been averted. Life and business would go on in recognizable forms.

The only major change from the previous twenty go-go years would be the trend rate of growth. The "new normal" economy was going to be sluggish for a while, five to ten years, maybe more, as the hangover from the multidecade debt party took its toll.

Shopatron's customers, one thousand branded manufacturers and more than twenty thousand retailers in ten countries, would be operating in this frustrating, slow growth world. They would face downward pressure on growth and profit margins, which meant that their decision-making behavior would undergo major changes. To compete, our customers would be sharpening their pencils, over and over again, for a decade or more.

Nothing less than a sea change was taking place in the economic world, and Shopatron was right in the middle of it.

POST-RECESSION STRATEGY FOR ECOMMERCE

Over the course of the spring and early summer months in 2009, I spent a lot of time contemplating how much the world was going to change over the next ten years. And what that would mean for e-Commerce. I reached a set of three conclusions:

First, the purchase decision-making process for customers of all types would place more emphasis on value versus price.

In a world where money is tight, people have less money to spend. Some people will respond by buying the cheapest option in the market, because they have no choice. But the middle-of-the-market customers will put higher weighting on quality versus price, because they are smart enough to do an analysis of what will pay off over the long term.

I call this cowboy wisdom. If you know you have only enough money to buy one pair of boots for the next ten years, you are going to make sure they are really good boots. Quality matters more when something is going to be used for a long time.

The second conclusion I reached was that customers (especially businesses) would have more appreciation for flexibility.

When money is tight, companies would tighten their belts. They would reduce staffing. Fewer people would be doing more work. These people were going to be more stressed and overworked.

This increased flow of work through each individual would result in more productivity, for sure. But it would also result in more rigidity and therefore more demand for inherently flexible solutions.

I call this travel delay wisdom.

Remember when the airlines were making tons of money, like twenty years ago? If you had a problem with your flight, it was easy to book onto the next flight. Today, if you miss your flight for any reason, especially during a peak period, you are going to be told that the next flight is overbooked, and the next one after that, too. You might be bumped to fly the next day or even the day after. This is because the airlines have gotten far more efficient at filling up all their empty seats, leaving no slack in the system if a plane full of people needs to be rebooked.

The same thing is happening in business today. Less availability to deal with changes to the operating plan, if something needs to change, and thus a need for flexible solutions.

The final conclusion I came to, when thinking about how the Great Recession would affect e-Commerce, was that communication was key, and good salesmanship would trump "relationship-building."

When times get tough, a natural resistance builds up in people, a resistance to spending money. I call this Darwinism. Anybody offering products for sale (including, of course, all of Shopatron's manufacturers and retailers), would encounter increased resistance in their customers. So how to sell to these customers?

In my life, I've read so many business books, I might just want to throw up thinking about the time I've spent. Most of them were a total waste of time, or could have been written in about 5 pages instead of 295. The most useless of all business books are sales books that push the idea that selling is really all about the relationship.

This is not true.

Selling is all about making sure the customer understands the benefits of your product versus the competition. And when the customer's guard is up, in the aftermath of a huge recession or just because she is having a bad day, she will care less about who sends her birthday congrats on Facebook and more about who is going to help her make payroll this month.

To sum up, my assessment of the new economic landscape resulted in Shopatron's post-recession strategy:

1. Emphasize value versus price in purchasing decisions.
2. Create flexible systems to counteract the effects of overworked staff.
3. Communicate benefits and value to customers.

A wave of cautious elation came over me. I realized something amazing had happened in my career. For the first time, I got incredibly lucky. My company, which I had been building for more than seven years at this point, was positioned ideally for this post recession reality.

1. Shopatron was offering an eCommerce solution that provided more business value than the competition's solutions. Better yet, it enabled our customers to, in turn, offer more value to their ultimate end-users.
2. Shopatron's software was 100 percent web-based, which meant that it was more flexible to configure than installed, licensed software. Our customers were going to love how easy it would be to manage.
3. Shopatron's retailer-integrated fulfillment solution helped our manufacturer clients to boost the effectiveness of their sales force and to sell more effectively to their customers—retailers and end-users.

Not only had Shopatron survived the economic storm, I felt like Forrest Gump. After a huge storm that destroyed or hobbled competitors, my shrimp boat was intact. We were ready to harvest the bounty of customers waiting for solutions just like ours.

Shopatron was a company in the right place at the right time to offer solutions to manufacturers and retailers in the post–Great Recession world.

SHOPATRON'S SOLUTION FOR MANUFACTURERS

If you ask my son who the manufacturer of his Xbox is, he would likely say "Microsoft." The name is printed on the machine. It's the brand that comes up on the screen when you turn it on to play. It's on every one of those $50 points cards we buy so he can stay at the gold or platinum level.

I think of Microsoft as a manufacturer, too. But the funny thing is that Microsoft, a "manufacturer," does not own very many factories. In fact, the vast majority of Microsoft's physical products are produced in factories owned by subcontractors in places like China. Microsoft itself does not make much, if making means metalworking, plastic injection molding, assembling, packaging, and the like.

If Microsoft doesn't "make" the Xbox, is Microsoft still the "manufacturer" of the Xbox?

I think so, because even if Microsoft isn't technically the company that assembles Xboxes and Surface tablets, they are the company that controls every single aspect of how those products are made.

A manufacturer is the company that controls the process of bringing a product into the market.

Using that definition, Shopatron has more than six hundred manufacturers as customers, who in turn sell more than one thousand brands. Some of them are small, selling as little as $250,000 worth of products per year. Others are large, multibillion dollar corporations with offices all around the world. Like UPS or FedEx, Shopatron works for manufacturers of all sizes.

No matter how small or big the manufacturer, all of them have been affected by the Great Recession. It's more difficult to grow now. In 2005 or 2006, if I asked any vice president of sales what her growth goals were for the coming year, she would always give me an answer in double digits. Now, even three years after the technical end of the recession, she would talk about low single-digit growth. She might even say "we're hoping to hold our own" as though zero or slightly negative growth was an achievement.

There are a couple of ways a manufacturer can grow faster, even in this slow growth economy. Developing a new product that everybody wants to buy—and for which there is no competition—that is a fantastic growth driver. But it's rare for most companies. Going to market with a portfolio of products that has competition is more typical.

At Shopatron, we can't help our customers make products better, but we can help them compete better online.

Shopatron is an eCommerce platform, and for most people in the world, that means that Shopatron provides websites and online stores that other companies (e.g., manufacturers) use to sell their own stuff online. We do have some nice website and online store technologies, which serve our small business merchants.

But we are famous for pioneering a transformational new concept, Allied to Win, which enables companies to join forces to increase sales, turn inventory, and deliver a superior and unique purchase experience to online shoppers. Shopatron's capabilities go well beyond what you could see on our clients' websites.

Manufacturers using Shopatron's model can take online orders at their website and have those orders fulfilled to the consumer via a dozen, a hundred, or even thousands of locations around the country. Our solution takes care of all the order processing: shopping cart and checkout (if the client doesn't have checkout in place at their website), customer notifications, payment processing, fraud control, customer service, and returns/exchange handling. We are not the cheapest eCommerce solution out there. But we deliver by far the most value for what we charge our customers.

In most cases, a manufacturer uses the Shopatron model to integrate its retailers (who are spread out across the country) as order fulfillment partners. It turns out that no other eCommerce company can provide this kind of capability to manufacturers.

It also turns out that fulfilling anywhere, from many locations, is one of the most valuable things a manufacturer can think of doing with their eCommerce program. Shopatron helps manufacturers sell more online.

First, it eliminates the conflict a manufacturer would have with its own retailers, if the manufacturer would sell at its website and ship directly to consumers itself.

I described this phenomenon in chapter 1, with the example of Johnny and his Herobrand running shoes. He went into the local store, got his stride analyzed and fitted for a new pair of running shoes, but then left the store and bought them online later. Even though Johnny purchased the shoes through the manufacturer's website, the local retailer got to make and fulfill the sale because Shopatron makes it possible for Herobrand to sell to consumers at their website while driving that customer back into the local shop.

And the benefits go beyond helping local store owners: partnering with retailers actually helps the manufacturer sell more because it removes barriers to doing business. A dirty little secret inside manufacturers who sell direct to consumers and compete with their retailers is this: marketing to consumers is constrained at every turn.

Promotions and consumer-oriented advertisements are held back, because they rub salt in the wound of the retailers who observe (as manufacturer-marketing activities increase) that the manufacturer is in fact competing with them. Not just picking up a few stragglers who come to the brand website.

When the Snakebrand's online marketing team starts sending e-mails to Johnny one month, two months later, inviting him to come back to buy at the Snakebrand store, that's when the trouble begins. Now the store owner, if he's paying attention, can see Snakebrand working to get Johnny to buy somewhere other than the local running store.

So the Snakebrand sales team (who is responsible for selling shoes to retailers) comes back to headquarters from the field and tells the marketing people to lay off the direct marketing because dealers are holding back purchases.

The net result?

Snakebrand's online marketing team gets their hands tied while Herobrand's online marketing team is free to market as much directly to consumers as they want. Herobrand's online sales go up. Snakebrand's go down.

Opening the floodgates on marketing is not the only advantage to integrating retailers as order fulfillment partners.

Shopatron's model also makes it possible to offer exciting new options for delivery to consumers. If Johnny wants to buy his shoes online at Herobrand's website, and then go into the local store the next day to pick them up, Shopatron can do that for him. In-store pickup of online orders increases sales for Herobrand because it gives Johnny more delivery experiences to match to his unique needs.

The Shopatron model helps manufacturers sell more in stores, too.

When retailers are engaged as partners, they are willing to invest more money in inventory. This is especially true when business conditions are tough.

Retailers, in the prerecession go-go years, often experienced double-digit growth. They were happy with their business, and they didn't pay as much attention to what manufacturers were doing on the brand websites. As long as the manufacturer supplied them with products on time, the manufacturer was good.

In times of slow economic growth, manufacturer's broader strategies and how they affect retailers get much more scrutiny. Retailers have more time on their hands to contemplate strategies, and they prefer manufacturers who are investing in retail distribution with the intent to put more stock on shelves.

Retailers respond to the emotional power of this message: "We, Herobrand, will help you turn that inventory sitting on your floor."

No matter how frustrating it may be to executives and private equity partners looking for magic bullet growth, there is no more capital-efficient way to grow a manufacturing business than through good old-fashioned retail distribution.

In this sense, Shopatron helps manufacturers turn more sales locally, thanks to retailers stocking more.

There are, however, a couple caveats worth mentioning.

First, in some industries the lines between manufacturer and retailer are quite blurred. Surf shops, for example, sell a ton of their own brand T-shirts. Has any human being ever been to Florida and not bought a Ron Jon surf shop T-shirt?

If I am a T-shirt manufacturer, I have to think of Ron Jon, at least in part, as a competitor. If it's OK for Ron Jon to be a manufacturer, then maybe it's OK for me to be a retailer and sell direct from my website?

Sure. Whatever works. Just keep in mind that salesmanship trumps relationship when you want to try to sell some of your inventory to Ron Jon. The buyer has the upper hand, and it's your job to sell. It's harder to sell when you are competing with your customer, but—as in all businesses—you need to figure out your own situation and create your own strategy.

Second, it is critical that the manufacturer's sales team use Shopatron solutions to sell more inventory to retailers. The sales rep needs to explain these value propositions to the retailer and show the retailer how stocking more of its products will result in more sales online and in stores. If the sales rep for Herobrand does nothing more than shake a retailer's hand and buy him lunch, the power of the Shopatron model will not be realized.

Thus, whether you are a manufacturer or retailer, salesmanship—the art of presenting value to a customer and helping him make a better decision for the long-term—is the key to winning more business, and Shopatron is poised to help with this.

SHOPATRON'S SOLUTION FOR RETAILERS

Retailers have a lot of incentive to listen to manufacturer salesmen who promise them an increase in sales. The economy is tough for retailers, too. When economic growth is slow, consumers' incomes can't increase much, and less income, of course, equals less money to spend.

Maybe people won't be saving wrapping paper like my great-grandmother did after her experience with the Great Depression, but retail customers are going to be more value conscious at every turn.

What's interesting for retailers is that, when value matters more to consumers, it's not simply enough to buy and put better value products on the shelves. Salesmanship itself becomes more important in the retail transaction because consumers often cannot see that one product will provide more long-term value than a similar-looking competitive product.

Take a simple purchase decision of picking between two power drills at Home Depot, for example. It's hard to know which of two similar-looking drills from two manufacturers will last longer, when looking at them in a superstore. Both are rugged looking, and the words "tough" and "durable" are printed large on their colorful boxes.

After two minutes of conversation, it's clear the guy working at Home Depot has no clue if one of these units is likely to last five years and the other one ten years. The quality of the motor, use of stainless steel instead of plated nickel in components, the type of plastic used. He's reading the boxes and pointing to them saying, "They both are pretty durable." His commentary is close to useless.

Go online and look at some reviews. There is some information, but it's superficial. One reviewer says he just got his drill and loves it. Five stars. Sounds like a planted review from somebody paid by the manufacturer—that is a lot more common than you think. Another guy says his battery doesn't seem to last long enough but otherwise the unit "seems well made." Seems well made? Really?

I'd like to see a review from someone who says "I am an electrician, and I've been using this drill for ten years. It has never let me down, even though I've dropped it countless times. My buddy has bought four crappy drills in the time

I've been using this single drill. I spent 50 percent more on this drill than the similar-looking cheaper competitor, but it has really lasted. I have gotten a great return on my investment over the last ten years."

In the store, a salesperson with just a tad bit of training and knowledge could approximate the helpfulness of such a reviewer. I just need a credible salesperson to tell me that one brand is far better quality than another. "A professional contractor would never buy this brand because it would fall apart after two months in the field. The pros all seem to buy this other brand."

And I'm sold.

Salesmanship trumps relationship.

Whatever a retailer does in the next ten years, it had better involve enhanced presentation of long-term value to customers.

One simple, albeit counterintuitive, way for a retailer to enable presenting more value to customers is to be a fulfillment partner for brands and manufacturers using Shopatron's order exchange.

Each sale received from Shopatron's order exchange is incremental to the sales that a retailer makes from its own advertising activities. Incremental sales are always profitable, since they require no additional overhead to make.

If a retailer is selling $500,000 a year today, and making $25,000 a year in net profit, then the addition of just $5,000 in sales from Shopatron (at a 50 percent gross margin) would add $2,500 to the net profit. This is an increase of 10 percent in profit for delivering $5,000 in incremental sales to local and regional consumers. To put this in perspective, $5,000 in sales at an average $100 per sale is fifty sales. Spread evenly over a year, that is about one additional sale per week.

With just one additional sale per week coming from Shopatron's order exchange, a retailer increases profits by 10 percent.

So what does that have to do with presenting value to consumers?

The 10 percent or $2,500 earned from incremental sales can be invested in activities that present value. It takes money to make money, right?

A small retailer could take $2,500 and spend it on sales training for staff. More engaged, credible store personnel can explain value propositions better to customers. This increases in-store sales.

Or, the $2,500 could be spent on a content-rich e-mail marketing campaign, which promotes the high quality of the products sold by the retailer.

A rich e-mail, packed with persuasive, sales-oriented content, is not trivial to produce. It costs time, money, or both. But—as customers are added to the e-mail list—each e-mail still takes the same amount of time to write. The photography costs the same. If a retailer has 1,000 customers on an e-mail list and adds fifty new customers from one year of Shopatron fulfillment activities, then the return on investment for all future e-mail marketing campaigns goes up 5 percent—like magic. Thus each additional customer grows a retailer's base for future marketing efforts and spreads the cost of sales and marketing activities.

Another way retailers can present value to customers is by leveraging the very existence of the physical store and the inventory in it. A retailer participating in Shopatron can become a local pickup point for online orders from manufacturer websites. Having a store near a customer can be a huge competitive advantage. And consumers use this service heavily; in most cases over 25 percent of online orders are picked up in local stores.

All things being equal, customers prefer to buy from a local store. They can touch and feel the product and alternatives. They can return or exchange the product instantly. They can connect with members of their community who share similar interests. They can purchase other items conveniently at the time of the pickup.

According to Shopatron's own research, more than 30 percent of online orders picked up in a store result in additional products being purchased by the customer. That's the kind of added value that makes a difference to retailers' overall profits.

Many large retailers, like Wal-Mart, Target, and Best Buy, have spent I-don't-know-how-many millions of dollars to put in-store pickup in place. Expensive, complicated custom software had been the traditional solution for retailers, but most don't have millions of dollars to spend on this kind of program.

When the recession hit, Shopatron started getting calls from sensible retailers who wanted to offer more delivery options to customers. Shopatron had a reputation for providing robust order management solutions at reasonable prices. They asked us if we would shift from providing order management solutions to manufacturers and begin to support retailers' own websites as well.

So, in a moment of recession fortune for Shopatron, we made a few tweaks to our software and began offering Shopatron Retailer, our solution for retailers' own websites.

With Shopatron Retailer, retailers can take all online orders, including those from their own website, and fulfill them from any distribution center or store location, which enables in-store pickup. These capabilities increase inventory efficiency and drive foot traffic into stores.

Besides being more cost efficient, Shopatron Retailer is more flexible than other solutions, too.

We help our customers save money by delivering them software over the Internet. Since the day we opened our doors in August 2001, Shopatron has always been a "cloud" solution. The flexibility inherent in the cloud model is a gigantic advantage for us and for our customers.

All of Shopatron's customers use the same, single system hosted on our servers. We configure it to work for each website as needed, but the software is the same for everyone.

If I were pitching a chain of twenty hardware and home supply stores, I might explain it like this:

Want to switch your flow of fulfillment so that lawnmowers now get fulfilled from local stores, while lawnmower blades will now get fulfilled by a third party drop ship supplier? Want to test the in-store pickup thing first and pilot just one lawnmower model being fulfilled locally, while the rest are delivered by freight carrier directly to the customer's address? Want to add a new fulfillment location, or take one offline temporarily? Or change a payment method accepted? Or set different return policies for different products?

All of these configurations are a matter of a phone call to Shopatron's support team, perhaps a day of setup and testing, and no charge whatsoever. For non-cloud software, you would need at minimum to file a request with IT and wait for a few weeks (or months) while they get around to making the change for you. Or more likely, you would call your order management consultant and three to four months (and ten or twenty thousand dollars) later, you would have your new order flows. Good luck if you want to change them back again.

A cloud-based order management system makes it incredibly easy to test and change business strategies, including expanding internationally. Add selling in Germany in a day. Or France. Italy. The UK.

No matter where you are in the world today, or whether you are a retailer or a branded manufacturer, flexibility to adapt to changing business needs is more important than ever.

It's been about five years since the financial crisis started and kicked off the Great Recession. As I reflect on those five years, I am amazed at the journey Shopatron has taken me through.

A confident young CEO raises $5.9 million in capital and brings on new investors. His company battles through the recession and emerges stronger and better positioned than he could have ever imagined. New consumer behaviors drive manufacturers and retailers to change the way they do business, and his company can provide the technology to make it happen.

Best of all, as a challenging economy grinds on businessmen and women for years to come, the company is able to serve customers with world-class solutions and yet remain affordable.

It all sounds so easy. So perfect.

Well, it wasn't. When you look at me today, as a human being, you will find a different person than you would have found in 2007. I cannot even recognize Ed Stevens of 2007. During the course of those five years, I encountered several personal and professional challenges that changed me forever and made me a better, more effective leader.

CHAPTER SIX
GROWING PAINS

Although I did not realize it, on January 1, 2008, or on any other day that year, almost everything I had learned about running Shopatron would need to be relearned.

The reason for this: a huge acceleration in growth. In 2008 when we began to invest the $5.9 million in new capital, our revenue grew from $3.5 million to $5 million—an increase of $1.5 million or more than 40 percent. Compare this to just a few years earlier in 2004, when our annual revenue was only $287,000.

Back in our early start-up days, Sean and I were poorly paid founders working in a corner of an unheated warehouse. We had committed the prime of our careers to building a business together and were willing to do whatever it took to succeed.

When a customer called Shopatron for support, we stopped the world for her. We gave each customer red carpet attention. We would listen, ask questions and get to the bottom of her problem. Then we would solve it—100 percent of the time.

Sean and I couldn't help but listen to each other talking on the phone. Each of us understood our software's weaknesses almost as if we were one person, and we discussed resolving problems with ease. Shopatron was going to be a great company, and we had limitless focus and energy to help it become that.

When Dave Dalrymple, a talented engineer, joined our team in November 2002, we began improving our software at a rapid pace. No meetings required. Just talk through the problem, then work and improve the product.

Customers loved the personal touch of Shopatron's service. They loved how quickly we improved the system, too. Best value ever, they would say.

Of course, it was a great value.

I didn't make a salary until 2004, and from 2004 to 2007 my salary was modest by any standard. Sean and Dave worked at much-reduced salaries until 2007 as well.

We were putting in long hours of great work, and we were not charging the company a market price for our time. The company could therefore sell its solutions at cheaper-than-market prices. Competing solutions were more expensive, because our competitors did not have employees willing to work for peanuts.

By 2004, we had too many customers onboard to manage ourselves, so we started hiring. Some great people joined the Shopatron team in those early years.

Daring. Entrepreneurial. Take a lower salary in exchange for some stock options. Help get the company off the ground.

These people worked closely with Sean, Dave, and me. I mean physically close. Eight people in a small room together, hearing each other's voices all day long. We were a close-knit operational bunch.

By early 2007, Shopatron had grown to thirty people working in a three-thousand-foot office. That was a number of people that Sean and I could manage without even knowing what management meant.

It was all working great—until we raised the $5.9 million I mentioned earlier to help us achieve three business objectives: (1) enter the European market, (2) increase investment in sales and marketing, and (3) develop in-store pickup solutions.

To make all this happen, we needed more people. Sales, operations, engineering, implementation, and finance.

It was straightforward to advertise jobs and hire people. Sean and I knew what our people needed to do, because we had done all of the jobs ourselves. As far as the type of people needed, we looked for experience. We wanted people who would hit the ground running on their first day.

To attract experienced people, Shopatron needed to offer an attractive career opportunity and a competitive compensation package. These new Shopatroners were not willing to put in three years of free work as I had done, or work for half a salary as Sean and Dave had done. To be honest, Sean, Dave, and I were not willing or able to work cheap anymore either.

By 2008, we had brought the company's average wages up to market levels. I didn't realize it at the time, but the shift up in wages was a major event in Shopatron's evolution. The company no longer had Sean, Dave, Ed, or anyone else subsidizing the daily cost of doing business. Shopatron's costs of serving each customer went up.

Higher personnel costs were not the only major change occurring at this time, though. Shopatron's employee count was fast approaching one hundred. The scale of our operation had surpassed Sean's and my abilities to manage it personally.

We hired salespeople who, without my direct coaching, never got up to speed. We paid them a salary month after month, yet they never sold enough to pay for themselves. Projects would get implemented at a loss because we had no way of tracking employees' time, and Sean couldn't oversee every project manager every day. Customers would call in to get help, and a founder was no longer available to assist.

The special sauce Sean and I had as founders could not be spread beyond our immediate surroundings, and neither one of us had experience in managing people in such large numbers.

We tried our best to make sense of the problems we encountered. Often as we dove into the details, we realized that one problem was really the combination of multiple problems.

For example, Sean and I lost direct connection with our clients, even our large ones, when we handed support over to an account management team. Even though the account managers we hired were good, caring people, they did not know Shopatron as well as Sean and I knew it. Clients, large and small, would sometimes call me directly and let me know that while they liked their account manager, the level of service at Shopatron had dropped.

We thought about the issue and decided the underlying problem was overloaded account managers. After all, we had been adding a lot of new customers. Our response was to hire more account managers, and this seemed to have solved the issue. Unfortunately, clients grew accustomed to the attention. Then later, as the Great Recession developed and we strove to become profitable, the extra costs in account management became a problem of their own.

We figured out that, for certain clients, we were spending more money on them than we were making from them. When we had to adjust their service level down, satisfaction dropped and customers became more critical of our software. If we weren't going to give them personal service to help manage our software, then they wanted us to give them better tools to serve themselves.

Fine. That all made sense. But this led to another problem: our engineering group over the years had not cultivated our software towards self-service. They had relied too much on manual support being available from our account management teams. We would need to go back and redevelop large parts of Shopatron software to enable self-service.

Cascading problems like this are common in growing companies. Some things that make sense as a small start-up (like relying on manual support) will not make sense as a big company (when self-service tools for customers are more efficient).

Ultimately, we did launch our European operation successfully, expand our sales and marketing presence, and become a leading provider of in-store pickup solutions, just as we had planned to do. Looking back, though, the most significant thing we accomplished with our $5.9 million in capital was transform Shopatron into a real growth company.

At a high level, this required a total overhaul of our business. We had to engineer a bigger business with hundreds of (more expensive) employees to deliver the same astonishing value to customers that we delivered when we were small.

Leading the company through this transition period goes down as one of the hardest things I have ever done. And, professionally, it has been the most rewarding.

How did I do it?

It was a lesson in discipline from the inside out. First, I re-engineered myself. Then I re-engineered the business, learning an entirely new language and toolset for management, metrics. Finally, I found the people and the core values to guide Shopatron into the future.

DISCIPLINING MYSELF

My dog, Ruby, loves to play fetch. If I say her name, she will not come to me. She will jump up, wag her tail, and initiate a frantic search for a toy.

When she finds a toy—any toy—she will drop it at my feet and look in my eyes with that tilted puppy dog face.

Ruby also loves to bark at birds—or whatever is passing in front of our house at the moment. A gentle old couple taking a walk. The neighbor's car. Wind.

Ruby loves to do whatever crosses her mind. She has no attention span. To prove to the world that she is a card-carrying member of the excited puppy club, she chases her own tail.

Most people are entertained by dogs like Ruby. It's fun to watch a fluffy white dog bounce from one thing to another without any care in the world.

And, if you think about it, it's fun to be that fluffy dog once in a while.

Turn off your brain and do whatever you want. Spontaneity is fun. Unstructured thinking. Timelessness.

Take a little trip and daydream.

My most innovative thoughts come to me when my brain is free of the constraints of time and space. Maybe it was the twenty-five Grateful Dead shows I went to while at Stanford. Or maybe I have always been that way.

It doesn't matter, because at age forty-four, I know I need to channel my inner Ruby in order to invent. To create.

Entrepreneurs like me love new ideas. New products. New anything.

I have endless energy for new ideas. My ideas. Your ideas. Ideas for me are like dog toys for Ruby. I'm always ready to grab one and play with it.

An idea is required to innovate—to do something that will change the world.

But—and this is important—ideas are dangerous. It takes a lot of time and energy (which in most businesses equals money) to bring a really good new idea to life.

Success is 1 percent inspiration and 99 percent perspiration. Thomas Edison, the greatest inventor of all time, said that.

One lesson I have learned about innovating: **If you are working to bring an idea to life, try not to get distracted with a new idea before the old idea is launched and making money for your company.** Otherwise, you have to write off all the time and money you spent on the old idea.

A distractible CEO launches and cancels projects without regard to the effect on staff morale or finances. It is not entertaining to investors, customers, or employees. Nobody has fun in a slow, bloated company that can't get anything interesting done.

For me, a CEO and yet an entrepreneur at heart, maintaining direction on current ideas while still saving time for listening to new ideas, is an essential skill. Acquiring this skill—keeping my inner Ruby in check—has been an evolving process for most of my life.

I have learned to put external controls on myself. I am married to a woman who adores simplicity and order. I give my operational executives considerable decision-making power and rarely intervene in their departments. I have financial partners in the business who guide me to avoid distractions and pitfalls.

These people have helped me discipline myself. And there is no way I would have gotten Shopatron to 2010 (our first year with over $10 million in revenue) without them.

As the company grew into "eight figures" of revenue, though, a strange thing happened. The velocity of ideas and information passing through my brain every day increased by an order of magnitude.

More new product possibilities. Input from a growing number of customers. New employees with hopes and dreams.

Random people would come up to me at Shopatron's trade show booth and tell me all about their company. Why the eCommerce landscape was changing. How they were going to help Shopatron. Prospective investors looking for companies to invest in would call me every week. The number of strategic options for Shopatron multiplied, then multiplied again, and again.

The external controls I had put in place—spouse, executives, investors—were no longer sufficient. There was too much information to even attempt to share with them. My entrepreneurial instinct was to listen to everything. Process it. Figure out what it meant.

It was the feeding tube of success, shoving ideas down my throat. And I had no idea what to do about it.

Then, one day in late April 2010, on an ordinary weekday evening when I arrived home from work, something extraordinary happened.

My daughter Lydia and son Colin were in the front room. Just thirteen and eleven years old, the two of them had arrived from swim practice a few minutes earlier.

I walked in on a discussion about triathlons.

One of the parents of a teammate had been training in the same pool with the kids that night. A fit fifty-something, he was getting ready for a triathlon.

Out of the blue, Lydia says, "Dad, you should do a triathlon."

"Yeah, maybe some day," I responded without delay and—being a practiced parent—without commitment.

I would rather put my head in a blender than go for run. I had not exercised in over ten years. I wasn't a bloated cow, but let's just say any six-pack I had was in the fridge.

Then, the surprise.

"If you do a triathlon, I will do it with you."

Hmm. Interesting.

But I did not say anything.

Then, the second surprise.

Colin says, "Yeah, I would do it with you, too."

It was a magical moment.

My favorite parental memory: the first time my kids inspired me. They were willing to do a triathlon just to help me to get healthy. Not many eleven- and thirteen-year-olds do triathlons, and mine were stepping up big time.

I had no choice but to say, "OK, let's do it."

In a most unexpected two minutes, my life—and I believe in some ways Shopatron's future—had changed.

A week later, I had read a few books and bought some quality running shoes at a local running store.

Overcoming the initial embarrassment of my first run—when everyone is thinking "Why doesn't that guy just walk?"—I persevered and went on to train six days a week for three straight months.

On August 29, 2010, I completed my first triathlon, the Santa Barbara Sprint. Colin and Lydia made good on their promise and finished the race with me. Robin joined in the fun, completing her first triathlon, too. The short course consisted of a five-hundred-meter swim, a six-mile bike, and a two-mile run.

One month later, I finished the Carpinteria Triathlon, which was a longer, Olympic distance race. The swim was one mile, the bike was twenty-four miles, and the run was six miles.

It didn't stop there. As of the summer of 2012, I had completed more than ten triathlons, including some famously challenging ones.

The hardest race I did, and the most rewarding to finish, was the Wildflower Olympic distance triathlon in 2012.

Set at the beautiful Lake San Antonio about an hour and a half north of San Luis Obispo, Wildflower is well known among triathletes.

For pain.

Peaceful oaks scattered among rolling golden hills provide the backdrop for hill-infested, leg- and lung-busting bike and run courses. I had done the race the year before and was curious to see what a year of training would do to my endurance and mental strength.

After a wardrobe malfunction fifteen minutes before the race which meant I had to safety pin my triathlon suit shut, I made it through the swim with no problems. But in the bike portion, just after the turnaround point on the ride at roughly mile thirteen, disaster struck. My right gear shifter came apart.

I had to stop. I got off the bike and repaired it best I could. I stepped back onto the bike, and then my right hamstring seized. Did someone just stick a kitchen knife in the back of my leg? I managed to hobble off the bike—for the second time—and stretch. I don't know how much time I lost—so many racers were zipping past me.

My repair looked good but wasn't perfect. For the remaining eleven miles of the ride, I had to hold my gear shifter in place in the gear I wanted. This meant I had to climb steep hills in my drop bars (in the aero position), which makes breathing deep difficult. Not a huge problem, though, and better than not finishing the race.

At least my safety-pinned triathlon suit was holding together.

Despite the problems on the bike, I managed to get back to transition two minutes faster than my bike time the previous year. In the asphalt-covered transition area, it was getting hot as noon approached. The temperature was in the mid-1980s.

Put on your running shoes, Ed. It's time for one of the world's most painful six-mile runs.

Before the race began, I had set a simple goal for the run portion: do not walk up the big ass hill.

In 2011, I was crushed by the bastard. Exhausted and overheated, I had walked up most of it in defeat.

Not this year, baby. I elevated my pain threshold and suffered to the top. I ran the whole way.

My heart rate hit 170 at mile three and never went below 170 for rest of the race.

I may have been on the verge of killing myself, but I did not walk. In fact, I sprinted the last 250 yards.

When I crossed the finish line, I collapsed, hunched over. I had shaved five minutes off my 2011 run time. Almost one minute per mile. A cold towel was placed on my head by a merciful volunteer. Regaining my composure, I sought something cold to drink and a chair in the finishers' tent. I sat there for twenty minutes without moving.

Overall, I finished the Wildflower triathlon 4 minutes faster than the previous year. Even though I experienced setbacks that day, I was clearly stronger than the year before.

I knew it.

I know it.

I know I am stronger than I have ever been, and not just physically.

To all those who doubt the power of exercise—and I was one of you—take it from me: physical fitness has translated into an intellectual fitness I could not have imagined. Six workouts a week hardened my Naval Academy resolve and distilled from me a mental discipline now essential to running Shopatron better.

I've learned that "I don't need to go for a run today" comes out of the same part of my brain as "I don't need to confront my vice president today about the low performance of his department."

One suffer-session at a time, I have trained that part of my brain to endure short term pain in exchange for long-term benefits. Someday, I will tell my kids that they sparked an innate love for triathlons. That they were instrumental in changing my life. That what started as an inspiration from them enabled me to take command of my most glaring weakness. That I had more control over myself, over my mind, than I ever imagined possible.

That mastering myself was the first step to mastering my business.

MAKING FRIENDS WITH NUMBERS

A train leaves Station A at 1 p.m. heading west at fifteen miles per hour. Another train leaves Station B at 1:15 p.m. heading east at twenty miles per hour on a parallel track. The trains will pass each other in 4 hours, 15 minutes. How far apart are the train stations?

A third train leaves Station B at 2:07 p.m., heading east at 142 miles per hour. When will the drunk engineer of the third train realize that he is going to ram into the other train and spew metal and noxious chemicals across the countryside?

Word problems: I hated them in elementary school. The math teachers from St. Michael's School in Independence, Ohio, were word-problem sadists—especially Sister Alaine. I think she liked watching the smoke come out of my ears as my brain overheated.

Or, maybe she knew solving word problems would be an essential life skill.

The single thing I dislike most about the universe—yes, the entire universe—and my life within it—is that I am required to solve dozens of word problems every single day as an adult.

I call it "doing the math."

In a typical day as CEO of Shopatron, word problems arrive fast and furious. The new programmer we want to hire is asking for either $2,000 additional salary or for a $3,000 moving allowance. That one is easy. If she stays at the company for more than eighteen months, the moving allowance is the better deal for the company.

Some word problems are so complicated it takes days or weeks to figure out what all the parts of the problem are. Often in those cases, we assemble and write things on a white board, the corporate descendant of the chalkboard. Conjuring Sister Alaine, I might ask in a meeting, "Would anyone like to go up to the board and write this down for the group?"

The first and most important thing when solving a problem is to understand as many variables of the problem as possible. In the early days of Shopatron, I would gather information by listening.

I would ask an employee what she was working on, how her day was going. Then I would ask her what kinds of things were causing problems in getting her job done, or what types of issues she thinks important for the company to solve.

If I was talking to a customer about a problem, I would ask as many questions as possible, always ending with the big one, "Is there anything Shopatron can do better for you?"

After listening to people describe problems, I would put together the word problem so it could be solved. It really was that simple for many years.

As the company grew to one hundred employees and more than five hundred customers, though, listening became less effective as a way to identify and analyze the most important problems. Ten people in the company, my direct reports and a few others had disproportional access to my ears. Their information became an interpretation of what other people in the company were telling them.

In meetings, the most eloquent speaker sounded smart, but his ideas might have been dumb. And in company-wide meetings, outspoken people talked while others stayed quiet.

Listening never stopped being important for me to learn about problems, but it lost 75 percent of its power as a management tool.

Fortunately for me, I have a helpful board of directors, and I speak with most members of the board regularly, often weekly. Also, I tend to be pretty honest about my problems and weaknesses.

A few board members suggested that we develop some quantitative ways of understanding our business. This way, they said, we could use numbers to tell us what was happening in certain departments. Metrics, they said, are used by all successful companies.

This made sense. Metrics are like sensors. You install a sensor somewhere and then use it to record activity. If a metric's reading goes off the chart, it is worth looking at.

Managing by numbers was a challenge for me, however similar to learning a new language. I had never measured anything about our business in eight years except revenue, profits, and cash flow.

We started by looking at a few simple metrics: cost per customer acquired, implementation margin, transaction processing margin, and account management costs vs. transaction revenue. These five metrics were excellent training wheels for the management team and me, and we started thinking about the business using numbers.

The hardest thing to absorb about metrics is that they don't have to be perfect measures to be perfectly useful. Even an imperfect metric, recorded quarter after quarter, will indicate trends. For example, our cost per customer acquired metric could never know exactly how much money we spent to acquire customers in a given quarter, because some new customers were approached one, two, or even three quarters ago.

Nevertheless, it is handy to see the trend of costs for signing each new customer. If they go up in too many quarters, then maybe we have some new competition or resistance in the market. If they go down, maybe a new targeting strategy is working.

Over time we learned that focusing on metrics allowed us to be actionable. **Metrics are a powerful tool for a growth company and can be used as a guide for making necessary changes in the business.**

After we got used to metrics, we decided to create a comprehensive executive dashboard. This included about thirty metrics from various parts of the business: operating costs per order, average recurring revenue per client, same store sales, accounts receivable analysis, and so on.

It took more than a year for the management team and board of directors to establish our dashboard and put it to use in the business.

Once we had developed the dashboard and committed to producing metrics on a regular basis (monthly, quarterly, etc.), we learned that producing reports took an astonishing amount of work every month. The executives could barely produce the reports even after hours of manual data manipulation in spreadsheets. Everyone had agreed metrics were important, but we were groaning under the number crunching and manual effort.

We decided to automate the production of our dashboard—and many other departmental metrics—in a business intelligence system. All of our metrics would get streamlined into a single reporting system, and managers would save hundreds of hours every year. The business intelligence system also would give us easy access to reports and allow for slicing and dicing of data.

Believe it or not, it took another year for Shopatron to get its business intelligence system from conception to full implementation. Budgets got in the way, as did executive priorities and bandwidth.

All told, it took us three years to transform Shopatron's management system from "let's ask everyone what they think" to "let's take a look at the data." Over those three years, there were countless times when the project could have gotten off track. We could have been looking back and joking that "running the business by spreadsheet" would probably have been a waste of time anyway.

But day by day, we made a little bit of progress. Just like training for a triathlon.

HIRING THE RIGHT PEOPLE

No chapter on a growth company's challenges would be complete without the biggest challenge of all: finding, retaining, and leading great people.

Despite the highly automated aspects of our business (black metal servers in cold rooms hum, blink, and click to make us money night and day), people are central to its success. The Shopatron system would not run for more than a few days without human fingers tapping keyboards to control it.

The importance of our people goes well beyond keeping the servers running, though. People are the drivers of innovation. They invent new and improved ways to manage online orders, so that our merchants sell more and shoppers are thrilled with each and every purchase experience.

The eCommerce business is dynamic, and our job is deliver the most innovative and cost-effective solutions to merchants. We must apply technology (millions of lines of software code and configurations) to meet the business needs of more than twenty thousand companies—and do this all within one single system.

Programmers, marketers, designers, writers, salesmen, implementers, accountants, and service agents all work together in symphony to deliver a remarkable range of capabilities to these customers. Plus, we deliver those capabilities in ten countries and in four languages. Thus human beings comprise almost two-thirds of Shopatron's operating expenses.

Just building a system like Shopatron and keeping it running would be a significant effort for any group of people. Yet we have one additional challenge: Shopatron can grow at rates of 30 percent or more per year. The system itself needs to be expanded and upgraded every year to keep up with rapid growth in user activity and transaction volumes.

Upgrading a complex software system at 30 percent growth rates is like rebuilding a jet airplane to handle 30 percent more passengers—while the airplane is flying at twenty-five thousand feet and four hundred miles per hour. The winds at high velocity are deafening. The machine rotates, rolls, and pitches as you work. Unexpected turbulence is possible anytime. Everyone on board is exhilarated and yet aware that one mistake could initiate a fatal crash and burn.

What a blast. I feel like I was put on the planet to manage this kind of stuff. There is no greater honor I could imagine than being the leader of a group of people willing to invest their life and energy into such a fantastic pursuit. Every day I go to work, I receive the gift of being able to work with dedicated, caring, and competent people.

The best gift I can give in return is to be the most effective leader possible. **With respect to employees, I've learned there are only three things that matter when building a company at a fast pace: (1) get the right people on your team, (2) get them in the right jobs, and (3) get them to work together with core values.**

Everything starts with hiring, which is not as simple as you might think.

In the early days of Shopatron, we used to think of hiring as a rational process.

Let's take filling an operations manager position as an example. We write a job description and talk about what our ideal candidate would look like. We put a start date in the budget. We review resumes and separate them into qualified and not qualified. As many Shopatroners as possible interview the best two or three candidates. Then somebody gets the job.

This process was comprehensive, and we still use most of it. However, it was flawed because it allowed the entire pool of candidates to be no better than just qualified.

The only thing that matters in a growth company is getting people who can hit the ground running. Everybody else slows the ship down. Bad hires cost the company a ton of money and make it hard to scale. For some reason, it's common for a manager to think that once they hire an inexperienced person as a development project, then the manager is no longer accountable for the results.

Now, after hiring too many mediocre people in Shopatron's early years, I realize that all the hard work in hiring is done at the very top of the funnel. We don't want to accept that the resumes we get are the resumes we need. If the candidates are not good enough, I stop the hiring process and push for better quality.

One easy way to identify an A player on a resume is commitment to success. There is no A player with a bunch of short stints. For a candidate with less than ten years' experience, I like to see at least two three-year stints mixed in there. Don't fall for the "bad luck" story, in which the candidate is a victim always stumbling into a dysfunctional company. An A player should have the ability to pick good employers. We don't want unlucky people working at Shopatron any more than we want incompetent ones.

Once we have hired someone, we do everything in our power to help them become successful. When circumstances change as the company grows and changes shape, our people adapt. Sometimes they have to upgrade their skills through training, and sometimes they need to change roles.

If a knowledgeable person can be moved into a position that suits her talents and the needs of the company better, I don't hesitate to move her. At the moment when I ask a person to take a new job that is out of his comfort zone, it is handy to have a company culture where people are not afraid to fail. Otherwise, I don't think he would take the risk.

Overall, to keep people fresh and enhance their knowledge of Shopatron, it's good to move them around the organization. At the executive level, for example, I have changed the organizational chart probably ten times in twelve years.

While hiring well and putting people in the right jobs at the right time are important aspects, it is critical to make sure all of these great individuals can work together as one team.

The way you get people to work together in a company with one hundred people in two offices on other ends of the planet is much different from how you do it in a company with eight people in the same room.

Company parties, all-hands meetings, and rewards programs all are effective ways to bring together people who might not even know each other's names. We deployed an internal social network (think of it as a Shopatron's private Facebook), which allows employees to chat, discuss topics, and share interesting links and pictures. We ran races together and created Shopatron jerseys.

While I believe these efforts have been effective in helping our people to work together, none of them has brought our people together as much as our company Vision, Mission, and Values.

A company's culture is the foundation of collaboration and innovation. Culture begins and ends with core values, codified or not. For the first ten years at Shopatron, our values had not been written down. When there are just a handful of people in an office, they know each other and know what to expect of each other. Behavior modification to fit in is normal in any small group.

When there are one hundred people, though, the natural instinct to fit in switches from fitting in to the whole company, to fitting in to the small group in which a person works. The programmers all start developing their own culture. The sales team forms its own culture. Each group becomes a siloed culture of its own. Then collaboration and innovation crash as the people in each group protect their culture at the cost of broader cooperation with other groups.

The only way to deal with this problem is to create a company-wide culture that everyone knows. Creating and disseminating company values is important because it enables all of the people inside a business to be part of the same group culture.

Great employees understand the power of groups, and they are willing to modify their own behavior to enhance results for everyone. But they do need to know the rules for working together. That's what values do. **Core values are important for a growth company. When presented in an authentic way, a company's values can help people understand how to do their job when there is no obvious way to do it**. Confused about how to prioritize your time? Look at the core values. Not sure how to react to a customer's complaint? Core values will tell you to get on your knees and apologize or to explain to the customer that they have not paid for the level of service they are requesting.

If I had to do one thing differently with this business, I would go back to 2001 and write down the company's values so they would be there during the entire transition from a garage start-up to the global enterprise we are today.

SHOPATRON'S CORE VALUES

Shopatron's Core Values are not only codified. They are written on wallet cards and distributed to each employee on his or her first day of work, along with a Core Values mug. We have Core Values posters for cubicles and conference rooms. Each and every applicant for a job fills out a Core Values questionnaire, in which they tell us what our Core Values mean to them.

It is fair to say that Shopatron's Core Values are as pervasive in our building as lights and carpet. And every bit as familiar.

Following is a summary of Shopatron's Core Values, those values that I believe are at the root of our success as a growth company:

Demonstrate Integrity
Always be honest and ethical in words and actions.

We demonstrate integrity by:

- Exhibiting a consistent character of honesty and reliability in our words and actions
- Dealing with our co-workers and customers in an honest and direct manner
- Proactively recognizing and acknowledging issues and faults
- Avoiding behaviors that would discredit the company

Integrity is not just about telling the truth. It's about taking responsibility for problems observed in the organization, owning an issue until it is resolved, standing up for what is right for our customers.

For example, if a technical support representative is talking with a client and learns of a bug in our system, she is expected to log the issue in our tracking system. On every Monday, we have an open meeting with the product and engineering teams to air out issues that need attention. That tech rep must come to the meeting and advocate in person that we fix this issue.

She must own that issue personally until it is resolved, even if it technically is not her responsibility to write software or to do quality assurance. Only she has visibility to the importance of the issue, and we rely on her integrity to see it through to resolution.

I don't care if giant corporations don't work like this. We do.

Be World-Class
Go above and beyond.

We demonstrate world-class values by:

- Achieving superior results
- Creating an environment that enables high-performance, satisfaction, and motivation

- Setting the highest standards and expectations
- Benchmarking against the best in the world

World-class products are built more by world-class teamwork than they are by world-class individuals. When challenges are encountered, the best people raise their game and never lose sight of the goal: excellence. They understand that the value of work is judged by the market response: sales, user adoption, and customer retention.

It is tempting to judge work based on tasks completed. I am building a car. I need wheels, an engine, an interior, etc. If I put together all the pieces on time and on budget, then my car project is a success, right?

No. The only thing that matters is that your car is actually the best car in its class, or at least a damn good second place. Task completion is no measure of success.

Keep It Simple
Make things easier for our customers and for us.
We keep it simple by:

- Taking extra time to design something that is simpler and easier for customers and staff to use
- Avoiding revenue opportunities that complicate our business
- Outsourcing when it's not core to our business and somebody else does it way better than we do it
- Avoiding the use of acronyms whenever possible

Often simplicity is overlooked as a way to create tremendous value for customers. Nobody likes complicated software that is hard to use. Be courageous and keep the feature list short—although often this requires more research and thought.

Often complexity comes through the door disguised as revenue. A big customer requests a custom feature and is willing to pay full tilt to get it. At first glance, it seems like a no-brainer. The project will boost both the top and bottom lines. And why risk disappointing a big customer by saying no to increasing the footprint of technology provided?

Because each and every custom modification and project carries with it long-term maintenance costs. A small company with ten engineers, for example, loses focus and the ability to innovate as the sheer overhead of the code base grows. Find an engineer with a reasonable head on her shoulders and listen to her when she tells you the project gives her the willies.

Finally, acronyms are insidious. Acronyms slow down communication between departments and make it difficult for new employees to understand the business. Acronyms are supposed to make things simpler to understand, but they don't.

Be Resourceful
Make the most of what we have.

We are resourceful by:

- Continuing to use equipment and technologies that function well, even if not fashionable
- Seeking low-cost solutions that get the job done
- Giving meaningful opportunities to inexperienced staff to grow and learn
- Spending money if it will save us money

When I lived in Russia, one of the engineers I worked with on the model engine project was Vadim Petrovich Kolobkov. A brilliant and funny man, Kolobkov was loved by everyone who knew him, including me. Kolobkov made his mark in the world by serving on the team of Russian scientists who put a man in space in the 1960s. He was the guy who designed the first space suit.

Russians are some of the most resourceful people on the planet, and Russian scientists are famous for their ingenious, reliable designs. Maybe it has something to do with evolving on a frozen tundra, maybe it is the educational system.

Kolobkov used to enjoy poking fun at American space engineers, whose designs were wasteful and expensive. He thought of NASA the way a poor kid working his way through college with two jobs thinks about the rich college kid driving his BMW from fraternity party to fraternity party.

While telling one of his space-era engineering tales, Kolobkov pointed out that, since there is no gravity in space, the ball-point pen would not work. So its astronauts could write in their logbooks, the Americans developed a pressurized "space pen" for roughly a million dollars.

Then he asked me what I thought the Russians did to solve the same problem. I had no idea.

Kolobkov lit a cigarette, offered me one as he always did, and picked up an ordinary pencil.

"These work in space, too," he said.

Be Helpful
Go the extra mile because it's the right thing to do.

We are helpful by:

- Listening to customers and assisting them until they are giving off the "happy vibe"
- Accepting responsibility for solving problems
- Working together with focus and alignment
- Giving constructive and positive feedback to each other, and accepting it as well

Being helpful isn't always an individual endeavor. Collaboration is the fundamental driver of innovation. And when it comes down to it, helpful actions are much more powerful than helpful words.

Put Family First
Taking care of those we love is our top priority.

We put family first by:

- Working productively during the normal workday to get everything done before it gets late
- Flexing when needed to be there for family
- Giving 100 percent at work because the company's success is the engine that provides financial security for our families
- Accepting and supporting each co-worker's family and lifestyle choices

Family First is not just about going home early to see your kid's soccer game. It *can* be about that, but that is too limited an understanding of the interplay between family and work.

The company's success in the marketplace is critical to providing the career opportunities our people need to provide for their families. We have to take care of the company because it is our source of money and growth, and sometimes this means making sacrifices, maybe missing a soccer game if the situation calls for it.

———

Over the last eleven years, I have seen Shopatron transform from a small start-up to a high-growth machine. My mental strength continues to improve through dedicated exercise and triathlon participation. My understanding of Shopatron grows as I use numbers and metrics to analyze and hone our operations. The Shopatron team gets tighter and stronger now that we hire more carefully and use our core values as a compass.

The systemization of Shopatron is not complete, but viewed from a high level, it is one of the main reasons why we are positioned to continue to grow 30 percent or more for the foreseeable future.

But this does not mean it has all been smooth sailing. Just after we began to find our groove and deal with the accelerated growth from financing, we faced our biggest crisis yet, or as I like to call it, the worst day of my life.

CHAPTER SEVEN
THE OUTAGE

The worst day of my life began like this: My alarm buzzed just after 5 a.m. I was too groggy to get out of bed. Since I don't believe in snooze, I rolled over into child's pose for a few minutes.

Child's pose, a downward-facing yoga position with knees to chest and face to the ground (or mattress), is guaranteed to wake you up. Maybe it's the stretching. Or perhaps the blood rushing into your head. Try it sometime. Your life will never be the same.

I've never fallen asleep in child's pose, and on the worst day of my life, after five minutes holding the position, I lifted up and staggered towards the kitchen. I wiped the crusties out of my eyes as I walked so they wouldn't fall into my coffee. That has happened before.

I prepped a fresh pot and hit the brew button.

Then I sat down at my kitchen table and opened my laptop. As the coffee brewed, I sat in my usual chair at the kitchen table. The table and chairs are from Ikea, fashioned from dark wood with stylish lines. I assembled them myself, as I did almost every piece of furniture in our house in 2008 when we remodeled and expanded our home from 1,100 to 1,650 square feet. The chair I sit in every morning is handsome but not comfortable.

It was Monday, December 14, 2009, and it was still dark outside.

On what would turn out to be the worst day of my life, I wasn't planning to write a book or compose important e-mails when I opened my laptop. I went directly to the Shopatron site we use for managing our business, the master administrative interface for the entire Shopatron system.

My foray into the Shopatron system was for enjoyment. I just wanted to look at order volumes, which are impressive in the holiday season and even more so on Mondays.

On this fateful day, though, I would not be pleased. Because when I asked my browser to pull up the interface, it told me Shopatron was not available.

I checked my web connection. Yahoo loaded normally. I attempted a refresh, but the Shopatron site could barely respond.

I refreshed again.

And again.

Nothing.

Something was wrong with Shopatron on one of the busiest online shopping days of the year.

Without hesitating, I picked up my cell phone and called Sean Collier, who was in charge of our server infrastructure. He had already spoken with Dave Dalrymple, our head of engineering. The damage assessment was not good.

"Two of the four nodes on the database cluster have crashed. It began with one node, and another one just went down. We have tried to bring them back up, but they won't restart. We don't know why they won't restart. That shouldn't happen. We are getting hit with peak traffic from the East Coast, and the remaining two nodes cannot handle it. They are going to crash very soon."

"OK. I'll be in the office shortly," I said.

I took a lightning-fast shower and grabbed something to eat in the car as I rushed out the door.

By the time I got into the office, before 7 a.m., Shopatron was down.

Not running slowly or responding with occasional errors.

Dead to the world.

No database. No Shopatron.

As I walked towards the engineering room to assess the situation in person, I glanced at my phone and checked for e-mails. No hate e-mails yet. The outage was just one hour old, and most clients had not noticed their online stores were not working.

Our engineers had noticed. They were sitting in a room that could hold about ten desks with computers and double monitors. Flow charts and snippets of code were written on the walls. Most of the engineers were staring at the screens and tapping away.

They didn't seem to notice I entered the room. They either pretended not to make eye contact with me, or they were too busy trying to save Shopatron.

Nelson Flores, a technical whiz from Chile who did most of our database work, was biting his fingernails.

I walked over to talk to him. Although I felt uncomfortable interrupting his furious keyboard strokes, I needed an update. "What's the latest news," I asked.

Nelson looked up at me and said, "The database is totally dead."

I paused and made sure my tone was positive yet firm. The engineers might have gotten us into this mess, but they were also the only ones who could get us out. There was no way of knowing what I would need to ask of them in the coming days.

"I understand. That's not good. What is our plan of action for getting it back up?" I asked.

"We are going to try to restart it again. If that doesn't work, we are going to need to restore from a backup."

My main purpose in talking to engineering was to make sure they were thinking clearly and making good decisions. Also, I needed to get information for the business guys, who needed to figure out what to tell customers.

"How long do you think that will take?"

"We're going to give it another fifteen minutes. If the restart doesn't work by then, we'll need three to four hours to restore from a backup."

Figuring it couldn't hurt to double-check that the engineers were communicating and coordinating their actions, I walked over to Dalrymple's office. As the head of engineering, he should have known what Nelson was up to.

He did, and he repeated what Flores had told me.

"We could try another restart, which is likely to fail, or we could begin to restore from backup. That would have us down until about noon, but it is likely to work. We'd like to restore from backup."

Dave sounded like he was thinking clearly. "OK, let's restore from backup," I said.

As I left the engineering area, I felt like every eyeball in the company was on me, looking for my reaction. Nobody could buy from any of our sites around the world. Tens of thousands of people were seeing "FATAL ERROR: Could not connect to database" on their computer screens. On one of the busiest shopping days of the year.

I tried to be calm and clear, keeping my words to minimum, focusing attention on the things we could do to improve our situation.

When all the managers had arrived at the office, around 8:30 a.m., I briefed them on the outage.

"Guys, the news is not good. Multiple attempts to restart the database have failed. The engineers are going to restore from backup, a process which takes three to four hours. This is a major setback; there is no other way to say it. We are going to need to work together as a team to make it through this.

"We need to get a communication out to customers. Account management needs to be briefed and reach out directly to their contacts as well. Customer service should be prepared for a lot of inbound activity."

Responsibilities were dished out, and the managers went to fight their fires.

After a quick check with Nelson on progress, I headed to my office and closed the door. I probably stared at my computer screen for an hour.

According to my e-mail records, at 9:32 a.m., I fired off a message to our board of directors. They needed to know that the database was down, and that their investment was in jeopardy. I felt it was crucial that they hear about it from me first. At a minimum proactive communication let them know I was in command of the ship.

Over the course of the next few hours, I watched my inbox as the shit hit the fan.

The first Board member to respond was Jay Kern, a thoughtful former McKinsey consultant and private equity guru. At 10:08 a.m. I got this e-mail from him:

HOLY @# percent$!
When you work through it perhaps we should have a call to discuss.

At 11:14 a.m., J. P. Whelan, Jay's partner, sent me this brief yet fair comment:

Totally unacceptable.

Then just five minutes later, an e-mail appeared from David Adams of Rivenrock Capital. David, at the time, was my third outside Board member.

I couldn't believe my eyes.

It was, after all, December 14, the five-year anniversary of our $500,000 Series A equity financing with Rivenrock Capital. As a condition of closing that deal, I had given them a right to redeem their stock upon the five-year anniversary of the financing.

In the midst of the database outage, Rivenrock was pulling the trigger and requesting Shopatron to buy back all of their stock.

Although we have long since resolved the redemption request (and as of 2013 Rivenrock was still an investor in Shopatron), on the day of the outage, this e-mail felt like a body blow. Less than two hours from telling him that the company was in crisis, my investor was heading for the exits.

I couldn't really process that at the time, so I forwarded the redemption request to our corporate attorney and moved on with my day. I didn't tell any of the management team, or Sean, about the redemption. Better to keep that one to myself and fight one battle at a time.

Around noon, I received more mortifying news.

Our first attempt to restore the database had been unsuccessful. The backup was corrupted and failed to start up at the same stage again.

Five hours of downtime, and we were back at square one.

"What do you think we should do at this point?" I asked Dalrymple.

"The best thing would be to restore an earlier complete backup."

At that time in Shopatron's history, full backups were created every four hours. Since the first backup had been made around 6 a.m., we needed to go back to 2 a.m. This meant that all of the orders and data that occurred between 2 a.m. and the outage around 7 a.m. would be lost.

The engineers told me that this would take another three to four hours. We would now be down until three or four o'clock in the afternoon—if that backup worked.

The next four hours passed in a flurry. Everyone did their best to see that the company was still operating. People were at their desks, taking phone calls from customers. The engineers were developing workarounds to capture orders without a functioning database. My predominant memory from the battle was and still is how honored I was to be the leader of such thoughtful and level-headed people. The troops were under fire and fighting hard. What more could I ask of them?

Before I knew it, at 4 p.m. the database was back up and running. We lost all the orders that were accepted from customers between the last backup at 2 a.m. and the time when the database died at around 7 a.m. But we were operational.

We were back on our feet. Foggy. Shaken. But standing.

I once again gathered the management team and reported to them that our systems were back on line.

A sigh of relief was on every single face.

No high fives or smiles.

Just relief.

Then everyone went back to work.

I stayed late that night to support the engineers by getting them food and encouraging them. They had a long night ahead of themselves to prepare for the next day. They had to figure out what made the database crash and how to prevent it again—all in about twelve hours before the next holiday rush hit us.

I also spent a lot of time that evening staring at my walls, at my computer, at the trees through my office window.

I didn't want to go home.

I just sat.

And worried.

The fear of losing everything coursed through my head over and over.

The regrets.

Should I have sold the business in 2006 when I had an offer for $20 million? If Shopatron doesn't make it, how will I rebound? How am I going to pay for Lydia and Colin to go to college? All of our college savings have been invested into this business. How am I going to tell Robin that our hopes and dreams for Shopatron might not come true? And forget about retirement—all of my retirement savings were tied up in Shopatron stock.

The brutality of business spares no unlucky bastard.

Damn. What a shitty goddamn day.

I glanced at the pictures on my file cabinet. My son was swinging a baseball bat in his cute little uniform. My daughter with her curly hair looked so happy and innocent as she forced one of those school-picture smiles.

Something about those photos hit a nerve. There was no way I was going to sit there and piss and moan. My blood pressure rose, and my mind cleared completely.

I have a lot more fight inside me, I thought. It's time to assess the situation and find the best path forward for Shopatron.

On the upside, we had avoided death by database failure. The backups did what they were supposed to do. I had a dozen engineers working through the night to repair the system. Shopatron was their baby, maybe a bit vulnerable at the moment, but they were going to protect it. The technology and broader system could be made stronger, after we investigated the incident and made improvements.

The management team did not freak out. Not a single voice was raised during the outage. No fingers were pointed. Everyone had fought well as a team and showed resiliency. I could count on my managers to stand together in the difficult weeks ahead.

The money we lost was measurable, but not a deathblow either. The holiday season is a good time to make money, and we would end up with an order spike on Tuesday as people returned to buy what they were looking for on Monday. There were 364 other days in the year. I didn't need to worry about financial consequences, at least in the short term.

The main concern I had was long-term client retention. Clients could vote with their feet and get a different eCommerce solution. The risk was that, after the holidays, they would add eCommerce platform replacement to their list of to-do's for the new year. A large exodus of clients could put a serious damper on our growth, especially since we were just coming out of the Great Recession.

Sitting at my desk late that night, I felt suddenly felt overcome with a sense of calm. It was clear to me now what the major risk was to Shopatron. And I knew what to do about it.

I got up from my desk, told the engineers I was heading home, and walked to my car in the chilly December air. When I arrived at my cozy little house in Pismo Beach, Robin had left the light on for me.

Despite the enormity of the day, I crawled into bed without the slightest fear of insomnia. I slept like a baby.

The next morning, I assembled the management team for a debrief on the outage. Our team agreed with my assessment that, together, we could mitigate a great deal of the risk of client fallout. We had been knocked down but not out. There was only one thing to do—get back on our feet and take action.

We focused our attention on client communication. I had read that a company can get a boost in customer satisfaction if it responds to a major failing in a sensitive and thoughtful way.

For starters, I wrote a heartfelt apology and sent it to all of our customers. It included details on the root causes of the incident and what we were doing to avoid similar problems in the future. It explained that we hired an outside technical consultant to review the Shopatron system and make recommendations on improving its reliability.

Our marketing team compiled a list of all of our customers and contacts. We broke down the list, which had perhaps 350 clients on it at the time, and assigned a segment to each executive.

Then, a Shopatron executive personally called and apologized to each and every one of our clients. While the calls required a significant amount of executive time, more than a thousand hours, I was confident that they were a great use of company resources. We could assess the magnitude of the risk of future client cancellations while at the same time reducing that very same risk through personal outreach from our most senior people. We also could explain in person that we were taking corrective action to improve Shopatron's technology systems.

At the end of each one of those client phone calls, we asked our customers one simple question: "What could Shopatron do better for you?"

This has always been my favorite question to ask customers—in the middle of a crisis or during a routine check-in. It elicits a simple snapshot of things customers want from me that I am not giving them. Also, it provides a framework for catharsis on known shortcomings.

Due to the recent outage, I expected customers to tell us that we could do better at operating our servers.

After completing our client phone calls—a few weeks later—the Shopatron management team gathered to discuss our findings. The results were surprising, to say the least.

A REVELATION ABOUT CUSTOMER EXPERIENCE

Don't get me wrong. Plenty of our clients were angry about the outage. They expected perfect website performance throughout the holiday season. The economy was just coming out of recession, and every single sale mattered.

At the same time, most clients expressed confidence that we would be able to upgrade our systems and avoid a similar outage in the future.

"I know your systems have operated perfectly for five years while I have been a customer, so I'm sure you can figure out what went wrong and fix it."

"I'm sure you did everything you could given the circumstances."

We even had some clients tell us that they were glad we were down for only fourteen hours.

"Shopatron is a key part of our strategy for growing both online and offline sales. We need you guys to be strong, and we're glad you're back up and running."

The support we received regarding the crash was remarkable. Yet there was plenty of negative feedback for us, too. When we asked our clients what we could do better for them, the chorus was loud and clear.

"Let me tell you where I really think you are going in the wrong direction."

"Here's what I really think you need to improve."

"This is where Shopatron needs to put more focus."

Client after client told us that the main thing we needed to do better for them had nothing to do with servers or routers. Software or hardware. Bits or bytes.

And it had everything to do with our commitment to giving shoppers a superior buying and fulfillment experience. Our clients wanted Shopatron to do one thing better for them: **customer experience**.

In hyper-competitive markets, manufacturers and retailers rely on their brands to differentiate their products. Give a shopper emotional value to supplement the practical value of a product; get a higher price (and a bigger profit margin) in return.

To support the overall goal of building a brand, the online shopping and fulfillment experience at a branded website should elevate the emotional value of a brand. Or at least not detract from it.

Much to my disdain, I had to admit in 2009 that Shopatron had a few quirks in our system that made things too complicated for shoppers wanting to buy from our clients' websites.

The worst violation of shopper convenience was how we handled identity verification in our fraud review process.

In 2009, when a customer's order surpassed certain thresholds and if there were other associated risk factors on his order, we would put his order on hold and send him an e-mail requesting a fax of his driver's license.

Forgetting about the fact that this process was completely unnecessary (we later abolished it), it was a huge pain in the neck for customers. It was, after all, 2009, and fax machines were not exactly common.

"Oh yeah, let me run down to the local copy shop and zip that fax off to you— or, wait a minute, why don't I just CANCEL MY ORDER."

In our post-outage survey of clients, we were reminded that the "fax in your driver's license" fraud process was stupid. But unlike previous times when clients told us this, our ears were calibrated for listening. Shopatron, because of the outage, was paying attention to customer needs like never before.

This was like a giant gift. In some ways, I had already been thinking that customer experience was something into which we needed to put more effort. And some of my executives, notably Brad Rubin in operations, had been consistent, strong advocates for improving Shopatron's customer experience. Even before the crash.

The feedback we received in our survey and a new consensus among executives cemented our strategic resolve. Instead of incremental improvements, we would go all in on customer experience.

It was January 2010, about a month after the outage.

I considered the options for transforming Shopatron into a leader in delivering superior customer experiences for online shoppers. The process, I estimated, would take years, not months.

Since the 2010 budget had already been baked (before the outage), there was no money allocated for improving customer experience in the coming year. Coming out of the recession and being fearful of a wave of client departures due to the outage, I did not think it was a good idea to go back to the Board and ask for a revised budget with higher spending.

At the same time, I did not want to kick off this effort with hot air and lip service. A big declaration—a company-wide "IMPORTANT" e-mail from the CEO—didn't feel like the right way to make real change happen. We were going to rebuild Shopatron around customer experience. This was going to take a hell of lot more than e-mail.

I decided to start with our people.

Shopatron had lots of smart, independent people. Some were strong advocates of customer experience and had already made that clear. Others were spiteful of customers and could not hide it. I needed to give the naysayers an opportunity to change themselves, and I needed to be prepared to ask them to leave the company if they didn't.

Building grass roots support and giving our new focus a foundation of authenticity became my goals for 2010. I spent a year explaining over and over, to my staff and then to every person at Shopatron, how customer experience was the most important thing for Shopatron's success.

When I traveled to our European office, I listened to countless suggestions on how we could make our application more user-friendly for our non-American customers. I steered the product development roadmap to include more projects to enhance the customer shopping experience. Besides eliminating the "fax in your driver's license" process, we smoothed the purchase path and made our checkout run twice as fast as before.

I co-authored a public statement of service excellence called the Shopatron Promise, in which we committed to system availability targets, service levels for our call center, and turnaround times for client requests. The Shopatron Promise communicated to our clients that we had heard their feedback after the outage. It didn't cost anything to produce—but it got the whole company thinking about serving customers better.

If I said the words "customer experience" once in 2010, I said them a thousand times. Little by little, we turned the ship.

By the time we got to the fall budget season in September, during which we would prepare the budget for 2011, my team had no doubts I was serious about this whole customer experience thing. They came to me in one-on-one meetings and confided that, while they understood this new and important goal, they were worried that they would not be given the people and money in 2011 to really move the ball forward with customer experience.

Operations wanted to staff deeper. Engineering wanted to invest more in quality assurance. The Product team wanted more people to figure out what customers wanted us to build and to make our application more usable.

I told them to put in their budget what they needed to improve customer experience. I would take care of the rest.

When all of the department budgets were consolidated, the result was ugly. Shopatron had made money in 2010, but thanks to all of the new investments in customer experience, we would be losing a considerable amount of money in 2011.

On Wednesday, November 3, the Shopatron Board of Directors met to review and discuss the 2011 budget. We met at Kern Whelan's office in the Financial District of San Francisco, not far from Chinatown. Unsure of what the board's reaction to major investments in customer experience would be, I had sent the budget to each board member in advance of the meeting and had called each of them to discuss the strategy behind the budget, and why it was so important for the long-term growth of the company.

My feeling heading into the board meeting was that they would support the budget. I was wrong, and after about thirty minutes into the meeting, all of Shopatron's outside board members (our investors) started throwing turds in my customer experience punchbowl. They felt we were overspending. Losing efficiencies. Maybe even being wasteful.

"We should be making money by now; this company is almost ten years old."

It was not the first time a Shopatron board meeting involved content-rich discussion on investment priorities. But this meeting was a bit more animated than most.

Normally, if all of my outside board members are making the same point, I will take a step back and listen carefully, and look for common ground on which to forge a consensus. This time I had to advocate my point of view without much compromise.

Customer experiences are either great or they are not. There is no such thing as a half-superior customer experience. There is no compromise.

I had spent an entire year telling my staff that customer experience was crucial to our success. I had reviewed their requests for money and people, and I knew we needed to spend money to get where we needed to be.

I remember thinking, "This is so important. This is what Shopatron needs to do. I am willing to lose my job over this."

We discussed management's requested investments in customer experience for the entire two hours leading up to lunch.

When the sandwiches arrived, there was a reprieve in our debate. The conversation shifted from the impassioned "I understand it is important for the company to make money" to the polite "Are there any turkey and avocado without cheese?" and "Could you please pass me a napkin?" The civility was reassuring and yet also uncomfortable. Nobody likes the feeling of disagreement in the air.

As we settled down to eat, loud cheering and shouting could be heard rising up from the streets below. The San Francisco Giants had won the World Series two days earlier, and the victory parade was passing one block from Kern Whelan's offices. The baseball fans on the board hopped outside to snap a few photos and take a break from the less celebratory atmosphere inside our conference room.

I wanted to see the parade but decided to stay at the table and discuss the budget further with individual board members as they filtered in and out of the room during lunch.

I was on my heels and needed to regain some composure. The board's negative reaction had surprised me, and I had not been mentally prepared for the discussion. Still, I knew our board members were good guys, and we all wanted the same thing for our business. There had to be a way to make customer experience central to our strategy and make the board members satisfied. I just couldn't think of how.

When we reassembled after lunch, Jay Kern said, in his usual quiet and confident manner, "Well, if investing in these customer experience initiatives is so important to the clients, then they should be willing to pay more for our solution. We need to take a look at a price increase."

It was a brilliant insight.

And I did not hesitate to agree.

"I believe passionately that customer experience is what we need to focus on, and I am willing to lose customers who don't think customer experience is critical to their success."

And that was that. It took about five minutes for all of us to agree that the management team would put together a proposal for increasing prices in early 2011.

SHOPATRON 3.0

Shopatron's annual holiday bash for employees and spouses, our Bah Humbug party, is held in January. With November and December being busy, at home and at the office, we like to celebrate together each year without the backdrop of social obligation and fatigue.

On Saturday, January 8, 2011, the theme for Shopatron's Bah Humbug party was fabulous Las Vegas gambling. Everyone dressed up in their finest (or silliest) nightclub fashions. Robin, my fun-loving wife, rocked an astonishing silver sequined dress. Others got in the spirit with suede and velvet jackets, stylish hats, and shiny shoes. We hired a gaming company to provide the tables, chips, and dealers. The rest, as they say, is history.

Although the theme was chosen by my assistant and her party-planning committee, quite independent from any strategic going-ons at Shopatron, we couldn't have been betting, eating, and drinking in a more fitting context.

Less than a month ahead, on February 2 to be exact, Shopatron would be making the biggest wager in its history.

After our board meeting in San Francisco, the management team had gathered, analyzed, discussed, reanalyzed, and decided. Improving customer experience meant more time was needed on projects. More staff were required to answer phones faster. An upgrade of the servers and technical infrastructure was essential for speeding the system's response times and for making it more robust and fault-tolerant.

To make these things happen, and more like them, our prices needed to rise 15 percent. No small amount. Without a doubt, our merchants and fulfillment partners would notice.

Would they remember that they told us to improve customer experience after the outage?

Did they expect us to provide a much higher level of service at the same price they had been used to paying?

Would we get a wave of pushback and threatened cancellations?

It felt like a huge gamble.

We wanted to mitigate the risk that we would be misunderstood, that our customers would think we were insensitive for raising prices as recovery from the Great Recession was just beginning. In our discussing how we would communicate the program to our customers, Mark Grondin, Shopatron's VP of marketing, and I decided it was worth hiring an agency to help us create the messaging and execute a campaign.

We engaged Whizbang Ideas, a small agency based in San Luis Obispo. Whizbang was run by Frank Scotti and Ellen Curtis, a friendly and creative couple who gave up their big advertising agency careers and moved to San Luis Obispo. Like many of us at Shopatron, Frank and Ellen wanted to raise their family in the Happiest City in America.

They sat in our conference room and listened to us talk about the outage and our new commitment to customer experience. After a few brainstorming sessions, we settled on a campaign called Shopatron 3.0. It was a no-nonsense campaign highlighting six aspects of Shopatron that had been and would continue to be improved. Efficiency for staff. Simplicity in pricing. Expanded customer support hours. Rewards for partners. Online marketing to drive sales. And richness in customer experience.

By using the 3.0 version moniker, we would communicate that this was indeed a new kind of Shopatron.

The centerpiece of the Shopatron 3.0 marketing campaign was a video. Four executives, including me, were to be filmed documentary style. We would share our passion for the upgrade to Shopatron; the video would capture it in our voices and on our faces.

Frank and Ellen gave us detailed instructions. Show up at the studio at 2 p.m. on Friday, January 7, 2011. Bring two to three extra shirts of various colors, so each executive would look distinctive and sharp on the screen. Study a set of questions in advance and practice your responses. Time is money in the studio.

The studio was located in a nondescript single-story commercial building, less than five hundred feet from the cold warehouse where Sean and I had given birth to Shopatron almost ten years earlier.

When I walked through the front door and into the small twenty-five-hundred-square-foot studio, it felt like I had stepped into a mini Hollywood: A camera and lights were pointing towards a single stool, surrounded by white light panels and reflective silver screens. A couple of workstations with big monitors for editing lined the walls. A table was set with bagels, cream cheese, and fruit for the crew.

There was a pretty, curvaceous woman wearing a black dress standing near a window. Next to her were a small chair and a table, and on the table was something that looked like a fishing tackle box. The box was opened, full of small things, but I couldn't tell what they were.

Frank greeted me.

"Hi, Ed. You are going to be taped first. So once you put your things down, head over to makeup so Bernadette can make you look pretty."

Right. I had forgotten about the makeup.

Putting on my bravest face, I walked over to Bernadette and introduced myself. A true professional, she asked me what I usually have done.

"I've never put on makeup before," I replied.

"Oh, goodie. That means I can do whatever I want!" she said in a sexy tone that—combined with a child's ice-cream-store excitement—briefly confused me. Then Bernadette got to work as the production crew bustled around us.

Meticulous penciling around my eyes. Some color on my cheeks. A little bit of this, and a little bit of that to accentuate my best features and correct my flaws.

Fifteen minutes later, when Bernadette finished perfecting my face, I walked over to the camera. I had never felt more confident. I couldn't wait to tell the world about Shopatron 3.0.

The taping went without a hitch. I had been thinking about improving customer experience for an entire year. I had repeated the messages to countless partners, employees, and customers. The words flowed uninhibited through my brighter-than-natural lips, and my enhanced eyes lit up. Sharing my vision in such a public way, in a video that would be viewed by thousands of people, energized me.

On February 2, 2011, we rolled out the Shopatron 3.0 campaign.

E-mails. The video. Phone calls. Letters. T-shirts. Meetings.

I traveled to industry shows, like Toy Fair in New York and the Snow Sports show in Denver, to speak with key clients. I wanted to hear the feedback and decide for myself if our big bet on customer experience was a winner or not.

Without an exception, our largest clients loved it. Or at least accepted it. They had the biggest, most valuable brands, and they understood the importance of premium experiences at their websites and were willing to pay for it.

Some of our smallest clients hated it. Customer experience didn't matter to them enough. Maybe it was because they were barely making ends meet, and they needed the cheapest eCommerce solution in the market. Maybe these brands were small *because* they didn't understand the value of customer experience.

In the end, no large clients and only a handful of small clients cancelled Shopatron. I was satisfied.

We had listened to our customers after the outage. We had built grassroots support for change within our own walls. We had gone to the board with our vision of the future. We found a way to meet the needs of our customers and our investors and shareholders. We crafted a campaign to communicate our vision for the future. And it worked. Shopatron 3.0 was a huge success.

MAKING IT STICK

After the Shopatron 3.0 campaign had run its course for six months, it would have been easy to declare final victory over bad customer experiences. I could have said, "Customer Experience. Been there. Improved it. What's the next big challenge for Ed Stevens and Shopatron?"

But I knew better. I recognized, by my original estimate, Shopatron was only halfway through the change process. We had at least a year and a half to go before customer experience was inseparable from the fabric of our company's culture. There was more weaving to be done.

We continued our investment in employee education. Front and center in our mission statement, we placed this sentence: We are passionate about making it easy for the best brands in the world to deliver superior customer experiences.

We printed fourteen sets of posters with our Vision, Mission, and Values written on them, and we hung them in every conference room, in the lobby, and in the hallways. We created wallet-sized versions and gave them to every employee, too.

On each new employee's first day, we started giving out a balloon on which it said, "I deliver superior customer experiences." I wanted our new employees to go home and, when asked how their first day at the new job was, say, "Great. I was really impressed with how important great customer experiences are to Shopatron. They even gave me a balloon!"

Since there really isn't a way to pay people more for giving great customer experiences, we found ways to show that we appreciate the extra effort it sometimes takes. Each month, we give a prestigious award called the Customer Experience Champion of the month, to one employee. The recipient is recognized company-wide for his or her outstanding efforts to serve customers. We give him or her another balloon. And, we give him or her for one month the best parking spot at our building.

We also give Customer Service Spot Awards. When Shopatroners go out of their way to help a customer, they can win a spontaneous thank you, a balloon (of course), and a $25 gift card of their choice: coffee shop, movies, juice bar, online music, or local department store. We have a gong that we carry out to the employee's desk and—if we are lucky—bang it before she turns around and realizes she is going to win an award. Surprised faces and laughs are priceless. While our people love getting recognized for great work, it gives me just as much pleasure to say "thank you." There is nothing like the feel good, win-win nature of a strong company culture.

It has taken patience and consistency to make customer experience a key focus for Shopatron employees. We started the change process three years ago, and we are still at work. The quest for superior customer experiences never ends.

But it never stops paying off either, resulting in happier clients, lower costs, and often more revenue as well.

In late 2011, for example, a leading consumer electronics manufacturer was running a national in-store pickup program with us. I received reports from our operational teams that the system wasn't working well—for shoppers.

There were too few locations available nationally. The process for authorizing retailers to become pickup locations was cumbersome. More than half of retailers who tried to enlist failed to get through the process.

We met with our client's sales force and talked about how to streamline the retailer signup process. Then we got to building it. Hundreds of hours of development later, we had built the world's most advanced national in-store pickup solution. We can launch a network of thousands of pickup locations in one day.

It was not easy to make it happen. In fact, it took one year from recognizing the problem to having it solved.

Our client was pleased that we met its needs in a decisive fashion. But there were benefits for Shopatron as well. We eliminated most of the human costs associated with launching a new pickup location on our fulfillment network. And by making it so easy to launch large numbers of locations, we opened the door to doing business with some of the biggest manufacturers and retailers in North America.

Thus Shopatron 3.0 lives on, and as a result of aligning Shopatron's strategy with the needs of customers, and staying on course in both actions and in words, we have found new engines for growth and strengthened our core business. Most of all, we are now positioned to look toward the future and develop our long-term vision for eCommerce.

CHAPTER EIGHT
READY FOR THE BIG STAGE

One day when I was a teenager, my mother told me in all seriousness that I was going to be famous. Not using vague or suggestive parental language, like "If you eat your vegetables and study hard, you can accomplish anything in the world you want." She said it like she really believed it.

The topic of my future came up because of a pile of astrology books and star charts on our kitchen table. Mom and her best friend Barbra Lustik were into reading stars for a couple years in the eighties. The two of them had been to an astrology seminar the night before. It was given by Buz Myers, an expert Cleveland-based astrologer. Buz was also a local celebrity, featured on TV to do the horoscopes. He had a soft and sweet voice that sounded trustworthy, and it didn't hurt that his hair made him look like Ted Koppel.

Mom relayed to me that the best part of the proceedings, without a doubt, was when Buz read some attendees' stars. Much to my mother's delight, he had read the stars of everyone in our seven-person family.

Buz had told my mom that the position of the planets and stars on my birthday made fame inevitable for me. Something about being a Scorpio with a Sagittarius ascendant.

As Mom recounted the story, she had no problem corroborating its prediction. "I guess that means you're going to be famous."

Not many parenting books would advise setting a child's expectation this high. And even fewer books would recommend doing so based on the interpretation of astrological charts.

But Janice Stevens was never one for books. She didn't get good grades. (My siblings and I were scandalized when we uncovered her crinkly, yellowed report card from Independence High School, with more than a few C's and a D or two.) Mom never went to college.

What Janice lacked in academic strength, though, she more than made up for with her powerful sense of intuition.

For example, when we would go on vacation, long before satellite navigation and smartphones existed, Janice was the family navigator. If we needed to find our way in an unfamiliar place, Mom could always do it. She would close her eyes, smell the air, think for a few seconds, and say, "Turn right. The museum is just over that way."

And it would be right where she said it would be.

Intuition is a powerful skill—more valuable than raw intellectual horse-power—in much of life and in most of business. In business, information that conveys a competitive advantage is de facto scarce. There isn't much to process that somebody else doesn't know.

When you do come across some unique information, you need to decide if you are going to put it to work, and if you do, timing is everything. And people who have great intuition just seem to get the timing right more often than others.

We've all heard entrepreneurs say, "It was a great product, just a bit before it's time" or "We hesitated to raise capital and a competitor overtook us before we could get to critical mass."

On the other hand, we have heard the stories of catching the perfect wave at the right time. Getting out of real estate right before the crash. Buying Google at the IPO. Toyota launching the Prius just as gas prices shot up.

A sense of timing and direction is a gift from God for any business strategist.

And in my case, it was a gift from my mother, too.

I always wondered about Buz Myer's prognosis, but for most of my life, and certainly the last fifteen years, it was hard to imagine becoming well known for anything. The struggles of starting and folding my first two companies and then the arduous launching of Shopatron wore out any sense of inevitability I might have had about making it big. Like many adults, by age thirty-five I had reset my expectations and my definition of success to (1) providing for a

130

comfortable, interesting life, (2) sending my kids to college, and (3) affording a decent retirement.

Thankfully, Shopatron did get to the point where it could support these basic expectations. Shopatron has grown at a double-digit rate every year since we started. We have more than seven hundred customers in ten countries. We process hundreds of millions of dollars of orders. We are a strong company with a platform that will last long into the future.

Among the thousands of start-up companies, formed by a founder's dreams yet never making it out of infancy, Shopatron has worked out well. It's an entrepreneurial success story.

Still, as solid as Shopatron growth has been, it hasn't been enough to make the fame prophecy come true. It hasn't been a real start-up rocket ship like Microsoft, Google, or Facebook.

The founders of these turbo growth companies become the legends of the start-up world. They make the cover of *Time* magazine in the year they go public. It would be fantastic to be Bill Gates, Sergey Brin, Larry Page, or Mark Zuckerberg, yet it would be lunacy to start a company expecting it to make you a legend, even if your mother told you that you'd be famous some day.

I always figured that Shopatron had as good a chance as any to make it to very large scale, but I never counted on it. Through Shopatron's eleven years, we have had some huge growth years and some less huge years. We have had some really successful new product offerings, and some we'd like to forget.

I've never stopped looking for opportunities to create a growth explosion, though.

One thing I love about business, perhaps more than anything else, is how fungible it is. One year's pace of growth does not carry over to the next. Innovation comes in fits and starts, and so do market opportunities.

Apple was founded in 1976 and grew like crazy for ten years. Steve Jobs was featured on the cover of *Time* magazine in 1982. He was forced out of the company three years later. The company went into an eleven-year period of stagnation from 1986 to 1997. In 1997, twenty-one years after being founded, the company almost went bankrupt if not for a $150 million investment by Microsoft. Jobs returned the same year. In 1998 the company launched the first of a long series of hit products, the iMac, which was followed by the groundbreaking iPod, iPhone, and iPad. Fifteen years later in 2012, Apple became the most valuable company in the world.

Rocket ship growth doesn't have to start on the day a company is formed and go straight up. A business can cruise along and then come across something big. Really big. All the entrepreneur has to do is see it. Adapt to it. Be the leader he needs to be. Position the company to accelerate.

And, as you can probably guess, I wouldn't have felt compelled to write a whole book about Shopatron if I didn't have a strong sense that Shopatron's engines were firing up and our business was lifting off rapidly to a new orbit.

It would be cool if I could say Buz Myers was right, but the important thing is not to become famous, but to do something that really matters in the world.

Shopatron is not going to invent a new way to derive green energy from plants. Nor are we going to find a cure for cancer, or even the common cold. No. We are going to transform the way people shop.

WHY SHOPPING MATTERS

I understand that at first glance it does not seem noble to change the world of shopping. But it is. Shopping is not just a frivolous activity like going to the mall with the girls and trying on things you don't really need. Killing time on a Saturday. Buying another pair of shoes.

Shopping is also what almost every person in the world does in order to feed and shelter himself. Shopping includes buying food, medicine, heaters, snow shovels, winter boots, plates, cups, forks, and knives. Of course, shopping includes buying fun stuff, too. But most of our money spent is on stuff we need.

Yet, not only does shopping take money, it takes time.

According to the United States Bureau of Labor and Statistics, which since 2003 has conducted a survey of time use, Americans fifteen years and older spent an average of 43.2 minutes shopping every single day in 2011.

Shopping takes a lot of our time: More time than we spend on food preparation and cleanup each day (33 minutes). And about the same amount of time we spend socializing and communicating with each other (42 minutes).

There may be shopping revolutionaries out there looking to get Americans deeper into credit card debt; I am not one of them. I just want to save people time when they shop.

Since the Internet has become a mainstream channel for shopping, a lot of time has been saved already.

The average number of minutes per day spent on shopping, 43.2 minutes, is actually an all-time low.

Since 2003, improvements in shopping technology have helped Americans save 5.4 minutes each day. To get a sense of what this means for an average person, let's do the math.

There were 247.5 million Americans above the age of fifteen in the 2010 census.

365 x 5 minutes saved = 1971 minutes / year / person.

This is 32.85 hours per person.

A 10 percent improvement in shopping efficiency was like giving every person in America an extra day a year, just by saving them five minutes of shopping a day.

There are a lot of ways to help people save time when they shop: More efficient product search capabilities. Better cash register technologies in the checkout aisle. Smarter store layouts. Informative packaging and product information.

Retail is a huge landscape, and no single company is responsible for the 10 percent drop in time spent shopping. Every company in retail strives to make things faster and more convenient for shoppers.

Shopatron's role is to help its clients, manufacturers, and retailers deliver superior (e.g. "faster") customer experiences. We do this by transforming online shoppers into active participants in the fulfillment of their online orders.

We give a customer options and control, then let her decide how she wants to craft her fulfillment experience.

Jane sees an ad in a magazine on an airplane. Maybe a friend recommends she check out a new product. Jane hits a search engine. Perhaps on her smart phone. Goes to the manufacturer's site directly. Or she finds a retailer who sells the product.

At some point along her research path, there is a moment of truth. The Jane-wants-to-get-this-thing moment.

Depending on what the item is, and on Jane's individual life circumstances, she is next going to think about how to satisfy her desire as efficiently as possible. Jane knows she wants to save time when she shops. She doesn't even have to think consciously about it.

If she wants to touch and feel the item before making a final commitment to purchase, she will want to see local inventory availability, store hours, and distance to locations. In a similar vein, she may want to purchase the item but pick it up in a local store, so she can explore accessorizing options.

The product could require special services such as assembly or installation of some kind. Perhaps it is a bicycle or a garbage disposal. Jane will need to know how much these extra services might cost, when she could have them performed, and who might provide them.

There is a good chance Jane might just decide to have the product shipped to her home where she will come home one day and find a brown box sitting on her doorstep.

Jane won't know which of these fulfillment scenarios might be needed until she finds the exact thing she wants to buy. Small nuances could sway her in one direction or another. For example, if Jane were buying a pair of shoes as a birthday present to herself, she might realize in the checkout process that she could wear them on her hot date Friday if the shoes were available locally. What started out as a ship-to-home situation changed to in-store pickup. Now if the shoes are not available locally, she might select another pair that is, because she just realized the shoes she has in her closet just won't do for the date.

For manufacturers and retailers who operate online stores, it is essential the store, shopping cart, and checkout can easily accommodate a variety of fulfillment options for customers like Jane.

And that is exactly what Shopatron does. We enable any set of fulfillment experiences to be offered in any type of shopping environment.

The product Jane wants will be made available to her at the time and the place she chooses. Jane saves time by having the control to craft the unique experience that works for her. She becomes an active participant in her order's processing.

Shopatron's vision statement says it all:

Any Product. Anytime. Anywhere.

We follow the Shopatron vision because it guides us to understand how tomorrow's purchasing experiences will evolve. As a big picture compass, our vision helps us to invest in the right technologies and to make good strategic decisions. Everything we do brings us closer to achieving our vision of time-saving, shopping nirvana.

CHANGING RETAIL ARCHETYPES

There are two kinds of forces we harness to drive Shopatron's vision forward: technology forces and social forces. I will start with the social forces, as they are the more important of the two.

Across retail, as it is with the rest of the world, the Internet is redrawing the social landscape. Archetypes that have lasted a hundred years or more—retail clerk as adviser, for example—are changing.

As information about product performance, business reputation, location, and brands are stored and exposed on the Internet, systems are evolving to package the information and monetize it. All for the benefit of shoppers who want to save time and money.

Giving online shoppers the ability to customize their fulfillment experience requires a system that stores and presents information about fulfillment and order processing options in every corner of a country.

If Jane is going to buy online from a national retailer and pick up her order at one of their nearby stores, each division and department of that retailer—from the eCommerce merchandising manager to the person standing at the customer service counter in the store—need to work together seamlessly.

When Jane finds a cool new exhaust for her motorcycle on the manufacturer website and wants to get it installed at a local dealer, the manufacturer and dealer are going to need to work together—using some kind of system.

Whatever it is, the system has to be large in scope, because many of the fulfillment experiences Jane wants require cooperation between two different businesses, perhaps three. There is likely an online player: marketplace, manufacturer, retailer, search engine, or ad network. There may also be a local player: a physical store or an installer. And, there may well be a third, an inventory center providing products from somewhere else in the country to the local fulfiller or shipping them directly to Jane.

It's mind boggling to think about managing all of these relationships. Who is going to make sure these various players work together to provide great customer experiences? How will margins be split, so each player makes his fair profit in each transaction? What happens when Jane wants to change her fulfillment experience midstream?

Somebody has to be the glue that holds it all together. Somebody has to make it easy for all these companies and channels to work together. And, if you haven't already guessed it, that's what Shopatron does better than any company in the world.

ALLIED TO WIN

As I mentioned earlier, Shopatron is the pioneer of a revolutionary commerce model. By breaking down the walls between manufacturers, retailers, inventory centers, online stores and local retail storefronts, Shopatron has over the past ten years dramatically expanded the delivery options for shoppers when they purchase online, including the ability to receive and return their orders in nearby retail locations.

To be fair, though, companies working together to serve customers is not something we invented at Shopatron. Amazon, for example, is an online retailer that works with more than one thousand vendors that drop ship products on its behalf.

Local stores and online retailers also are working together to enable in-store pickup and installation. Tirerack.com, for example, is the dominant force in the online tire business. It has a network of thousands of independent installers across America who put tires sold by Tirerack.com onto local customers' cars.

But as far as I know, we are the only company which views the cooperation between trading partners and channels as *the* essential ingredient to meeting customer needs in the future. And the amount of cooperation we see between retailers and manufacturers and between online and offline channels today is just a small taste of what is to come.

For one, we will see continued expansion of all the types of alliances we see today. Ultimately, every single retailer will bring its channels together to offer buy online, pickup in-store. All of them will expose their inventory onto the web for customers to find easily. Every manufacturer will expand the "dealer locator" function on their website to become a "product locator," which will identify the exact locations of a desired product within any geographical region.

Also, businesses will form many other kinds of alliances, creating altogether new experiences for shoppers. Marketplaces like eBay will take orders for in-store pickup at any location the customer chooses. They do this for some big retailers today. They will eventually need to do it for all retailers.

The system for buying products locally will need to improve. While many sites provide local search capabilities, nobody cares about local search that can't guarantee an immediate fulfillment experience. Search engines will need to provide more robust local fulfillment capabilities to complement product search.

Retailers will continue to pull inventory from vendors to sell online, but they will layer in delivery of this inventory to stores for in-store pickup. A sporting goods retailer will offer a complete range of kayaks that can be picked up in a local store, for example.

All of these new ways of working together will be driven by customer demand. In most cases, the demand will be to save time. In other cases, it will be to save money on shipping or other services required.

Alliances are useful for companies because they help meet customer needs in a more efficient way. Alliances help companies win.

When companies become allies in commerce, they can reduce the amount of capital investment required to enable flexible fulfillment scenarios. Sharing store inventory means reducing inventory-carrying costs. Partnering with other companies that already have the inventory nearer customers is more efficient than putting more of the same products on the ground to serve the same market.

Cooperating with another company in a transaction does mean sharing some of the revenue and profit. As long as such cooperation makes it clear to the customer who is ultimately in charge of the overall experience and who should be contacted if service is required, it makes sense even for competitors to work together. An alliance allows each company to get one-half of a sale rather than zero halves of a sale.

And this kind of cooperation elevates the customer's experience when she is face-to-face with your brand. You can't build brand by trying to sell something to a customer that she doesn't need or want. Better to find the exact item and get it to her as soon as possible. Don't try telling her how she should receive the product, either.

True engagement is too damn precious not to make a lasting, positive impression.

Airlines, perhaps the most challenging of all consumer-driven businesses, have known this for years. If you are delayed due to some fault of the airline, and they don't have a reasonable alternate flight, they will rebook you on another flight—from a competitor. They will pay a competitor to fly you home.

While at first glance it would seem no competitor should ever be willing to help another, both competitors know that an alliance serves both of their brands better.

Airlines have taken cooperation even further. Consider the Star Alliance. I can book a flight on US Airways or United out of San Luis Obispo, California, and get frequent flier miles into the same account. These are the only two airlines that serve our local airport, and therefore they compete for my business.

US Airways and United websites will sell me tickets on each other's planes, even if there are competing routes. Convenience (the best departure and arrival times) is paramount to making the sale and, when I am traveling, is a major factor on my overall experience.

Thanks to ever-rising customer expectations, alliances will continue to propagate. Beyond what we see from airlines. Beyond what we see among manufacturers and retailers today. And at the center of many of those alliances will be the easy-to-deploy connector technologies of Shopatron.

OUR FUTURE

Everyone knows that an iPhone—inherently—is a complicated piece of technology. Processor, memory, touch screen, speaker, microphone, accelerometer, and software (of all kinds). Metal, plastic, glass, buttons, cords, adapters, and batteries. Few companies in the world, and even fewer individuals, could ever imagine making an iPhone from scratch. There must be thousands upon tens of thousands of engineering hours invested in every new iPhone model.

Yet as intricate and complex as it is, the iPhone is most famous for being simple. Does anyone need an instruction manual to use one? I watch a three year-old playing with an iPhone and think, this is the essence of complex technology made easy.

Every tech company including Shopatron has something to learn from Apple. We want our platform to be as straightforward to use as an iPhone.

For the most part, we are succeeding. Shopatron today offers the simplest way to launch the kind of fulfillment programs needed in the omni-channel era. For example, we can launch a national in-store pickup program for a manufacturer or a retailer in just one day. No other technology company I know of can even come close to that.

As we move into the future, I believe Shopatron will lead the way in omni-channel fulfillment—offering the best solution for brands all over the world to deliver superior customer experiences. We have been working towards this vision and, thanks to our technology, people, and company culture, are uniquely positioned to see it come true. Here's how:

1. Shopatron has superior, multi-tenant technology

Shopatron is—and always has been—a 100 percent multi-tenant system. Worldwide, we have only one set of software code, which serves all of our customers' order management needs.

In this way, Shopatron is like Google. When you go to Google, your search request is handled by the same software as my search request. Google didn't make a search engine specially for you and host it for you. It built a big search system, and you use it along with the rest of the world.

Multi-tenant architecture is the most efficient design for software. Sometimes it is called "software as a service" (or, if you have to use acronyms, "SaaS") to distinguish it from a copy of software you license and install onto a machine for your exclusive use.

A multi-tenant solution is massively more cost-effective than a single installation of software. Regarding network infrastructure, there is one set of routers and firewalls to maintain. Each added security measure benefits all customers. Configurations and equipment are more robust: global, faster, and safer.

Upgrades are automatically available to all users of the system. When Google publishes a new feature to their search engine, you just get it. There is no need to install anything on your computer or phone. No need to even lift a finger. Same with Shopatron.

If one of our customers wants to launch an in-store pickup program, we could do it for him same day by making a simple configuration to his account. It is that easy.

Also, our solution is based in the cloud, making it easier to access. Anywhere there is Internet connectivity, your application is available for use. We pre-build connectors (called APIs) to the most popular platforms and service providers, such as gift card providers, payment processors, and shipping companies. We maintain each connector one time and spread the benefit of reduced maintenance costs across all one thousand brands using Shopatron.

Thanks to the economies of scale of a multi-tenant solution, the total cost of ownership over any time period is lower than with old, legacy systems. Often 50 percent lower.

While there are plenty of unscrupulous legacy software companies selling their single-tenant solutions as having the "benefits of SaaS," it is important to keep in mind that "SaaS" has come to mean "hosted on the web." And being hosted on the web does not provide cost savings unless solution itself is multi-tenant as it is at Shopatron (all customers of the software company use the same application on the same code base).

And as I touched on in Chapter 5, some of the legacy providers got into the business of handling order fulfillment for the big retailers, like Wal-Mart, Target, and Home Depot. When huge national retailers wanted to launch in-store pickup programs, they turned to big technology companies such as IBM or Oracle to provide the software.

If you consider the quality of customer experiences at these retailers, for the most part the big tech companies and their services partners did a good job. I don't know how much any of these goliath retailers spent on launching in-store pickup, but I would bet a pretty penny it was in the tens of millions of dollars.

That's right. Expensive.

And, if for that money those retailers got a system that was easy and low-cost to maintain, it might have been a great deal. But now if they want to make a change to or add a fulfillment experience, like adding ship-from-store or changing the process flow, it is going to be an expensive project that could take a year or more to budget, build, and deploy.

And probably another million dollars or two.

Complex, single-tenant solutions, whether hosted on-premise or hosted on the web, are too costly. Only big retailers seem to be able to afford to spend millions on software that behaves like concrete poured into a business.

What companies need in today's challenging economy is software that helps them meet consumer needs while improving profitability as well. Software that doesn't just add costs and maintenance burdens and slow down the speed of doing business.

Shopatron enables more types of delivery experiences with more companies than any technology provider on the planet, in an easy-to-deploy multi-tenant system. We eliminate technology limitations so business decision makers can spend their time and budgets on giving shoppers what they really want.

2. Shopatron's technology is not only superior— it's patented.

As recounted in this book, it took years of sacrifice and risk to bring my vision for eCommerce to life with Shopatron. To help protect my enormous personal investment, I applied for a patent on a system and method for processing product orders. Today we call this technology the Shopatron Order Exchange. One of Shopatron's early board of directors, Paul Arlton, helped me write the initial patent. We believed the ideas underlying the business were groundbreaking, and we wanted to be rewarded for the time and effort required to prove the ideas were valuable.

In 2013, after a longer-than-anticipated review process, my patent application was approved. I must have read the e-mail from our attorney twenty-five times. I was jubilant and danced around the office high-fiving anyone who walked by. A patent would make it that much clearer to manufacturers and retailers that Shopatron was offering a unique and valuable solution.

Shopatron's patented Order Exchange makes it easy and affordable to deploy advanced fulfillment models like in-store pickup, drop-ship, ship-to-store and ship-from-store across a retail store network. The Order Exchange removes cost and complexity and creates easy connections of channels and trading partners.

The most important element of the Order Exchange is that it works equally well with fulfillment partners who can provide inventory information and with those who cannot. Because it can work without inventory data, Shopatron's

Order Exchange also has more robust failsafe capabilities when inventory information is available but not error-free.

Shopatron's patented, cloud-based Order Exchange allows manufacturers and retailers to ally together and win, to seamlessly leverage the available inventory of every retail storefront and distribution center when fulfilling online orders. Only Shopatron offers the full range of fulfillment options needed in today's competitive market.

That's what Allied to Win is all about.

3. Shopatron offers economy of scale by serving companies of all sizes.

To make good on the promise of "Any Product—Anytime—Anywhere," we need to include the products of small, niche manufacturers, and make in-store pickup available in the location most convenient to a shopper—even if that location is a small independent retailer.

As an industry veteran, Shopatron has always served both large and small companies, in the same way that United Parcel Service will ship a million packages for Amazon or a single package for my grandmother.

Most technology companies are unable to serve very small and very large customers at the same time. IBM, in the eCommerce sphere, serves only the largest manufacturers and retailers. It's not just IBM. Many companies that make websites are specialized according to client size. It is rare (maybe impossible) to find a small retailer and a big multinational brand using the same eCommerce agency.

Allied to Win is different, though, because it involves managing orders *after* they have been placed by the online shopper. It requires a mind-boggling number of connections between thousands of websites and tens of thousands of fulfillment locations, which creates real-world logistics like shipping, payment processing, and store operations staff.

And in any logistics scenario, scale matters a lot. The costs of managing each individual order drops notably as the scale of the processing system grows.

Combined with the economies of scale of our multi-tenant system, Shopatron's large footprint of customers and fulfillment locations means we have a scale that other companies cannot duplicate easily. For this reason, we can provide a better solution at a far lower cost than anyone else in the market.

4. Shopatron's secret weapon is its culture.

A company culture is difficult to build and even more difficult to duplicate. At Shopatron, we have a unique culture that is the result of eleven years of concentrated efforts building our business model and developing our core values.

Shopatroners are a special bunch of people. We understand the importance of details yet, above all, we focus on bringing simplicity and order into the world. We help each other and our customers to learn and grow as markets shift. We look for clever, cost-effective solutions to problems. We strive to produce results that are world-class. We care about the people who touch our lives. We are open and honest with ourselves and our customers.

All of this adds up to a resilient and powerful force that drives better customer experiences for online shoppers. Our honest approach to business, perhaps most of all our core values, gives us a competitive advantage.

In today's omni-channel landscape, transparency is king. Taking a complex logistics scenario and making it simple requires an open dialogue between stakeholders. Our customers must know we are guiding them towards better solutions rather than looking to optimize our own revenue or profitability from each and every interaction.

If you are going to be a force for bringing companies and people together, if you are going to be a uniter, you have to have impeccable reputation. The best way to build a large company with a reputation for honesty and integrity is to leverage power of culture.

Our location in San Luis Obispo, California, is a huge plus for our company culture. A small town with forty-five thousand full-time residents is the type of place where relationships matter. People who appreciate bumping into neighbors at the local farmer's market hang their hats in SLO town. Leave the world a little bit better than it was when you were born unto it. There are a lot of people in SLO whose life ambition is that easy to summarize.

A small town location is also conducive to long-term employee retention. To find the talent and skills to continue growing our company, we hire young (often from the local university) and promote from within. We make a special effort to bring in consultants and trainers with broad experience to teach and train our people.

Because they tend to work with us for a long time, our employees care about the long-term consequences of customer interactions. Shopatron employees have the knowledge and perspective to avoid common pitfalls in launching complex fulfillment scenarios. They will likely be supporting the manufacturer or retailer for years to come; there is every incentive to deliver solutions that will be easy to maintain and operate over time.

By bringing all of these strengths together, our patented technology, the benefits of significant scale, and the efforts of our dedicated workforce, Shopatron is able to create commerce alliances better than anyone else in the world.

And we will continue to make our vision a reality, bringing together companies and channels for the betterment of shoppers: saving people time and money, making manufacturers and retailers more competitive.

Leading the eCommerce industry from the front.

CONCLUSION

Shopatron came to be through a combination of unique circumstances and pure willpower.

It all starts when I am born into a family of entrepreneurs and learn not just how to sell products, but also how to take chances. A stint in the navy provides leadership training. After living in post–Cold War Russia, I marry a woman who can handle all the risk and sacrifice of start-up life at least as well I as can.

An idea to use the power of the Internet to connect companies and help them serve customers more efficiently emerges. I am crazy enough to bet the farm and start a company. Countless family, friends, and investors tell me the Shopatron concept, Allied to Win, won't work.

Obstacles present themselves: recessions, growing pains, system crashes. My team members and I overcome each and every one. We survive. We grow. We innovate.

After eleven years, market forces coalesce in alignment with our vision and Shopatron gets a chance to make it onto the big stage.

I wrote this book to share the story of an entrepreneur and his company's path to creating a groundbreaking eCommerce solution. To help all of Shopatron's new employees and customers understand our vision, core values and dedication to customer experience. To tell the world that we are doing something they need to know about. To inspire others to take a chance and build something new of their own.

And while there are a few things I might do differently if I had to do them again, all in all, it has been a pretty good run.

But it's dangerous to rest on past laurels. Contentment dulls an entrepreneur's edge.

Better to seek a state of unrest. Aspire to create something new.

With the same excitement I had on that first day walking onto the grounds of the Naval Academy as an eighteen-year-old boy, I look forward to the future and wonder what challenges lie ahead.

EPILOGUE

When a submarine is cruising across the ocean, every twelve hours or so the boat ascends from the depths up to roughly thirty feet below the surface. At this depth, it is possible to make radio contact with fleet commanders, get instructions, and advise them of your position. Also, the ship takes on much-needed fresh air.

The ship has a huge snorkel that rises up from the sail like a periscope and sticks up through the water's surface. The snorkel can pull in fresh air and push out stale air from the entire sub, all in the course of a few minutes.

Back on the USS *Cincinnati* during my midshipman duty, after we had passed Bermuda, we realized we were getting close to home. Training concluded, and the mood on the boat shifted. Whenever we would go up and get some fresh air, somebody in the control room would ask the officer of the deck if he saw Norfolk, Virginia, yet through the periscope.

Everyone was thinking about getting home.

"What are you going to do when you get home?"

That was the question.

That was always the question in the last thirty-six hours of our voyage.

Take the kids to Disney World. Buy a new car. Get engaged. Go drinking with buddies in New York. Visit Mom and Dad. Have sex for two weeks straight.

If there were a gauge in the control room that from zero to one hundred measured crew enthusiasm for arriving at a destination, it would have read "0" during our travel and training from Gibraltar to Bermuda. With three days to go, the Arrival Excitement Gauge picked up to thirty.

With just two days to go, all the fresh food had been consumed. We drank canned milk and ate canned vegetables. No problem. Cleaning orders were given. The ship was scrubbed inside from top to bottom, so admirals coming on board would be pleased. Even though the cleaning was tedious, nobody cared. Arrival Excitement was now running at fifty, more than enough to energize us.

On the last day at sea, I woke up for a helmsman shift that began at 6 a.m. The timing of my duty was superb because the ship was just entering the Chesapeake Bay when I took the controls. We were already on the surface. Land was already in sight. The control room was quiet; most of the crew was still sleeping.

Command after command, turn after turn. There were a lot of course changes, as we navigated towards the naval yards.

Once we got within a few miles of the docks, around noon, my shift was over. The timing could not have been better. The Arrival Excitement Gauge pushed up past ninety. The bridge had a dozen or more people standing around doing nothing. Technically, hanging around the bridge is forbidden. Only working sailors are allowed. These mostly senior sailors knew the rules were bent on arrival day, and nobody asked them to leave. I had been on shift, so I just found a corner, stood quietly out of the way, and observed the climax.

The Arrival Excitement Gauge was at ninety-five.

Through the periscope, the dock was spotted. Sailors, including me, took turns looking through the scope. About five hundred yards in the distance, with a destroyer parked to the left and three other submarines lined up to the right, was our dock. On it was a crowd of people. Is that a marching band over on the right? There must be a thousand balloons.

At this point, the Arrival Excitement Gauge was pegged at one hundred. Tough men who had threatened to strangle the captain to death were now quivering and smiling like ten-year-old boys.

"I think I see my kids."

"That looks like my wife."

"Is that a marine standing next to her with his hands on her ass?"

"Shut up, dick-head, it's my turn on the scope."

The ship moved slowly towards the dock. A few men went on deck to handle the lines. Thirty minutes later, we were secured. Music could be heard coming down through the sail, through the hatch, into the bridge.

I climbed up the ladder onto the deck. Glancing over the scene, I saw a dozen World War II victory posters. A man walking across the plank in uniform. A woman spotting him from the dock. First hurried steps then running. A huge embrace and an endless kiss.

A little girl standing and looking up at her parents. The big sailor bends down grinning and swoops her into his arms like she's a teddy bear. He holds her and twists around in circles as her legs fly.

The band played, one happy anthem after another.

There was no Arrival Excitement Gauge on the dock. Just the joy of lovers and families. The joy of humanity.

Get your flags. Wave them wide and high. A successful deployment. We are all safe.

The USS *Cincinnati* stood silently behind all of this. Once a protector and war machine, now just a black canvas for the celebratory scene.

The captain stood on the deck, no wife or children nearby. He had pushed his crew, some would say too far. All that was forgiven, or at least forgotten. His job was to accomplish a mission and get these men home.

He said to me, as he looked over the jubilant crowd, "Son, this is why we become officers."

APPENDIX

ONLINE RESOURCES

Website for this book:

alliedtowin.com

Additional stories that I didn't have room to tell in the book:

alliedtowin.com/blog

"My Latest Startup is a Corporate Rugby Team:"

alliedtowin.com/rugby

Additional photos:

alliedtowin.com/photos

Book recommendations:

alliedtowin.com/books

Follow me on Twitter:

twitter.com/eastevens

More information about Shopatron:

ecommerce.shopatron.com

Shopatron job opportunities:

ecommerce.shopatron.com/careers

ACKNOWLEDGMENTS

I would like to thank my mom and dad, Janice and Cliff Stevens, for giving me a stable and safe home from which I could take risks. Also thanks to Robin, my wife and true friend, who, despite having hundreds or maybe thousands of justifiable opportunities, only once or twice verbally doubted my ability to make Shopatron work. Thanks to Colin and Lydia for being good kids who kept mid-afternoon emergency calls from teachers to a minimum. I don't think my wife or kids have ever really complained when I needed to work late or travel—and that is a true blessing for an entrepreneur.

No dedication would be complete without thanking Sean Collier. Sean taught me how to get things done, and he never minded doing the dirty work. If you ever get to choose the guy who will be in your foxhole, choose Sean.

Thanks to Paul Arlton, a longtime customer of mine at Norvel and the most honest and nice person I have ever met. He's a damn smart engineer, too.

Thank you to my siblings Cliff, Cindi, Pete, and Joe. I love you and know you must have had a pretty big effect on how I turned out.

I wouldn't want to forget my mother- and father-in-law, Russ and Blyth Carpenter. Your book writings in part inspired me to write my own story down.

Also thank you to my buddies Andy Erickson, Seth Streeter, Mark Herthel, Gordon Miller, Mike Chesser, Rick Stollmeyer, Mike Mansbach, Jason Kelly, and Bill Borgsmiller. There are more than a few great business leaders on that list, and I am privileged to have had the opportunity to learn from each of you.

To all of Shopatron's early supporters: Thank you. Thank you. Thank you. A healthy dose of trust can fuel a guy like me for a good long time. I am thinking about Elliot Epstein, Ted Frankel, the Broberg Family, and many, many others.

Thank you to the board members and financial partners who delivered a great deal of value to me and to Shopatron: Jay Kern and J. P. Whelan of Kern Whelan Capital, David Adams and John Nelson of Rivenrock Capital, and John Witchel.

A huge thank you to the people who inspired me in my early years with their wisdom and confidence: Irina Barnes, Professor Schupbach, and Professor Ivanov at Stanford University, Professor White at the Naval Academy, and Tom Sege.

Finally, I would like to thank all of my colleagues at Shopatron who drive our vision forward every day.

A good number of my accomplishments are really those of others.